Memoirs
Of A
Sherwood Miner

By
Trevor Maddison

Memoirs Of A Sherwood Miner

Edition: 1

Copyright © 2019 by Trevor Maddison

DEDICATION

I dedicate this book to my grandad, Eric Swanwick, who has long since passed away in the mid-1980s, and my Grandma, Mini, his wife, who followed him just six weeks later. She was the most perfect Grandma that any boisterous child as I was could ever hope to have, along with my siblings who were equally loved and cherished by them. Eric was an Overman from Thoresby Colliery, but he did time in the mines working from the ground up to what was probably the highest level a working man could normally expect to achieve in the British coal mines. In truth I only came to understand what Eric had done for us when I entered mining myself and learned first-hand what a tough world it is. Thank you for your love that meant so much back then, and still does.

Title: Memoirs Of A Sherwood Miner
Genre: Factual, Popular History
Author: Trevor Maddison

Synopsis:
Mining is not just a job, it's a way of life and a culture. And it is also a war. Not a war against man, but against nature, and Mother Nature can be a formidable foe. Almost everything we need to survive we must retrieve from the ground – minerals we call them. Someone has to do it. Miners are the ones who meet that challenge head on and in so doing nature invariably fights back and takes her toll. Mining is almost universally seen as the most dangerous job in the world, and for good reason. Here the author pulls no punches. For those that do it the risks are ever present. It is perhaps that raw sense of risk and living life on the edge that breeds the kind of men that these memoirs are about.

The author grew up in a mining community near the idyllic surroundings of Sherwood Forest, so his story is not just about the mining industry, but about life with the surreal contrast between these two extremes – beautiful countryside, and the dirty, grimy experience of descending daily into the bowels of the earth to earn a crust. Why do miners choose to do it? Well, for the most part they were born to it, and it is just what has to be done. But, as for those who go to war, life for a miner is not dull. The men that do it are feisty and energetic, with a raw but very rich sense of humour that comes out in their culture that is a frequent topic in these memoirs. Modern mining is a huge tram effort. It is about technology and it is an audacious adventure where working relationships are needed to meet the challenge. That's where this story gets really interesting – in meeting the men and communities that have formed around the industry for centuries. It also includes episodes where all of that energy came to clash with the government of the day in the form of the yearlong miner's strike in 1984/5 where Nottinghamshire played a key and controversial role.

The author grew up in the distinguished country village of Edwinstowe, Nottinghamshire and began his career in 1977 at a very special mine nearby – Thoresby Colliery. It is special because it is located in a world famous region known for its legend of heroic outlaws, but also for the lesser known reason that Thoresby Colliery was probably the most successful deep coal mine is Europe and for that reason it was the very last in the UK to close in July 2015, on the 55th birthday of the author it so happens. But this is not about just one mine. It is about the whole of the Nottinghamshire coalfield and the national and international industry as a whole. As a nationalised industry the training of its management was extensive so those that took the challenge went through nearly a decade of preparation where they saw all aspects of the industry from top bottom. That is the background of the author, so his experience is probably as broad as it could be. He was also an engineer, and so closely involved with the ever advancing technology of the mines, so these aspects do get some focus. War these day is not just won with men but with machines, and the same is emphatically true of mining. We live in a technological world. For those that grew up in mining this book will be a pleasant walk down memory lane – though a muddy grimy lane at that. For those that grew up outside it will be like a glimpse of a life that is perhaps almost as alien as visitors from Mars. Enjoy.

TABLE OF CONTENTS

PREFACE

There came a time when I realised that in terms of my life as a miner, who grew up around Sherwood Forest, I have something really interesting to share, both in terms of the region and the industry. The mining communities I grew up in are still thriving, but the mines have now all closed. For those of us that worked there, the memory is unforgettable. And so in fact is the culture. As the saying goes 'You can take the lad out of the pit, but you can't take the pit out of the lad'. In my view that's a good thing, despite what others may mean by it.

I decided to write partly for the benefit of those that live in these cultures and communities, with a history of mining, who never worked at a mine themselves. To give them a view into the world of their parents, grandparents and ancestors in some cases. A view they would probably not otherwise get other than by word of mouth from their relatives who used to work in the mines. But I am also writing to remind the miners themselves of what incredible days they were, and possibly to give them a broader view of their own industry from my unique experience of it.

I wondered whether to write chronologically and give you some definite sequence to my experience. That would perhaps be the natural thing for me. I also wondered about covering it category by category – men, technology, history, culture, humour, danger etc. But in the end I decided to just mix it up. After all, variety is the spice of life. For most of us we are not the kind of people who eat our Yorkshire puds first; then the mash; then the peas etc. We like to mix it up a bit; it just tastes better that way. Of course we all know someone that likes their world more ordered like this, even one pea at a time sometimes, and if that's you then I must apologise and say I did it this way by what I perceive to be a majority decision, in keeping with typical union policy, just to keep it as spicy and interesting as possible. What that means is I will jump forwards and backwards, almost at random, sometimes even into my childhood as this too was part of my story and my experience, and my preparation for working in the mines. So the events I describe did not necessarily happen in the order I write them, but they will in some way be relevant to the aspects of my experience I am writing about in its place. I hope you enjoy it this way. What you should find is your overall picture of my life will emerge as from a fog as I come to fill you in further on parts of my memories that I only touched on in other places. When it comes to the chapters, what that means is there is no real logical split. All of the chapters jump around quite a bit, so all they do is break the book up a bit into manageable sections that will allow you to take a break and grab a much earned bite or two of 'snap', along with a nice hot cup of tea ready for the next chapter.

Though these are largely my memoirs of my mining experience, what I am sharing is much broader than that. These are the memoirs of my life. The circumstances that led me into mining – the community I lived in, the locality, my childhood, my particular influences in life, my life beyond mining etc. are all very individual and these events and conditions don't all apply to everyone that made their way into the industry. We each have our own path through life. Those details are all part of my personal story. In some ways they are typical, but in other ways very unique to me. Some of it is very unusual so those parts shouldn't be taken as the common experience but as one that deviates from the norm. I will be sharing all of this – the circumstances and events that have made my life what it is. After all it is these personal details that make exploring another's life so interesting; by it we discover how different the experience of another is to our own. I don't intend to sanitise it much either. Every life story includes trials, troubles and conflict. There are dark times, mistakes, grief, sorrows and sometimes tragedy. If that is not true then let's face it – not much happened did it? My life has all of this, as well as the good times we all like to remember, but a life story is not complete without it. For me it has not all been 'plain sailing' by any means; or maybe I should say not all 'plain digging' as that would probably be a better metaphor for a miner and land-lubber like me. All that said, I don't have regrets. Even the bad experiences form us and make us what we are. Maybe I would reverse some of it if I had another chance, but living with it as my past is not a problem for me because I have an optimistic view of life, that nothing is wasted.

One particular detail of my experience of mining is that I was an engineer – trained by the industry over a period of nine years, and educated under sponsorship of the industry at a local university. That gives me a unique viewpoint, but a good one because mining in the modern world IS engineering. It is not just a battle of men but of machines, as is true for much of this modern technological world. To make those machines work for you is really now the greater part of the challenge. We have inherited a world where we are the taskmasters of machines, but they can be as rebellious and troublesome as any human, and at times they can turn on us and exact the ultimate penalty if we don't treat them with respect. There lies the greatest danger of mining in our modern world, so welcome to the modern 'pit' that is not that far removed from the bear pits of old and they share something of the same kind of historical infamy.

CHAPTER 1

Who was it that said 'I think, therefore I am'. But he never worked down a pit did he?

I come from a breed that knows they are alive first and foremost because they have lived a physical life, and a demanding one at that. Mining is physical, there is no other way to say it. But it doesn't stop there. It is also psychologically demanding and it can tax every faculty of the human soul. While Descartes with his pithy maxim may choose a cerebral existence, it is primarily for physical reasons a miner knows he's alive, and I reckon this is the more true the nearer he gets to the coalface. Every department of his being must be active and aware to succeed and survive.

Some would consider mining to be an unnatural thing; to burrow away in the bowels of the earth like that. But when you think about it we all started life in a very confined and wet environment, from which we had to tunnel our way out through a very narrow channel to escape, all accompanied by blood, sweat and tears. The experts even call it a 'canal' – an industrial term for sure. They were clearly thinking along the same lines that I am, so we all had industrial beginnings of a sort. Yes, mining is a much more of a natural thing than most people suppose. In truth we were all born minors (pardon the pun). In some ways it takes us back to our very roots. Ok, I admit there are some key differences between mining and the whole birthing thing, but there are similarities too you must admit.

My actual mining days began age 17 when I left school. But they really began much earlier than that because I was raised in villages that had a mining culture – the villages of

Edwinstowe and Ollerton in North Nottinghamshire – my home, so my exposure to what mining was and is began not when in August of 1977 I signed up with the then UK National Coal Board (or NCB), but with my first exposure to that mining culture even as a child. I was actually born in the village of Edwinstowe on Abbey Road which is on a former council estate. In those days, when I were a lad, hospitals were a luxury. I was delivered at my home by the local legend Nurse Norton that did the same favour for many of us that emerged there.

Since I left the industry ten years later, in my latter years I lived further afield and got exposure to other British cultures ranging from cities, to the coast of Devon, to the middle class areas of Surrey and Hampshire, including time spent in the big smoke itself; London. One thing I discovered was our fellow countrymen from the south think anything above the Watford Gap is 'North', and some are under the illusion you need a passport to go there. Why? Because it's full of foreigners – northerners, like me. Not true of course (and I'm a Midlander really) but there is no question there is a culture gap between many parts of the south and the mining communities such as the one I grew up in; a culture that 'southerners' sometimes find particularly hard to understand fully, or break into.

Those Midlands roots persist in me sustained by one immutable fact – my accent. Wherever I go in the UK people know roughly where I am from. Not all can pinpoint it exactly, but they generally have a good idea about it. I never attempted to change that. I am proud of my roots so why should I want to change it? One thing I have observed about the UK is that the broader accents tend to stick for life – Scottish, Yorkshire, Scouse, Brummy, Geordie all usually retain their accent as do others. Notice I didn't list Nottinghamshire there. That is because the accent in the county is generally a little softer than those mentioned and I find that usually means they don't retain it as much but adapt to wherever they go. However, the mining communities tend to be a little more isolated than their counties as a whole and so the accents are a little broader and tend to stick more than the norm. If you want to hear a really broad accent, go to a county where the accent is already broad and find a mining village there; though if you do I suggest you take an interpreter with you. Over time I met many miners that came down to the Nottinghamshire coalfields from the coalfields in the North – Durham, or Ayrshire and the like. When they first arrived communication was best limited to hand signals because in terms of language it would have been as easy had they come from Mars. We all adapted though and in time, whether it was them that changed or us, we soon began to sing from the same hymn sheet. That said I can't ever remember a native Geordie coming out with the local signature phrase 'Eyup Duck', even if some Nottinghamshire guys did become quite fond of the Geordie expression 'Wae'aye man', so maybe it was us locals that turned a little bit Geordie after all.

My birth place and the place most of my life was lived, as I already mentioned, was in a village of about 5000 people called Edwinstowe in North Nottinghamshire. Most villages of this size wouldn't have too much of a national or international profile, but Edwinstowe is a little different for a number of reasons. First because it sits at the very centre of Sherwood Forest which has a famous oak tree known as the *Major Oak*. A large tree for sure but not the largest oak tree in the country, though certainly one of the most famous because of its Robin Hood connection. That is a little ironic of course because in the days we understand to be those of Robin Hood, whoever he was, the tree would have been a mere sapling. Or to be completely accurate, it would have been three saplings because it is in fact three acorns grown together to make one very large and unusual tree. In fact the Major Oak stands majestically in a very attractive tract of forest full of antique oak trees, up to 1000 years old, that are a real part of our national heritage. Each tree is a unique work of art each with their own form. Many of them are known by their form as 'stag oaks' given they are partly dead and often show bare upper branches that resemble the antlers of a stag – a phenomenon that is not fully understood, though there are a few theories on how it happened. The UK does in fact have a legacy of oak trees that exceeds the whole of Europe put together, many of which were planted by the Normans who first came here to Britain in 1066 AD and became the new ruling class. It also goes back to the days when oak was used to make ships, so these trees were the very security of the nation, reserved for building ships, along with the many Yew trees planted around the country specifically for the making of longbows – another Sherwood Forest theme.

The longbow was an advanced and terrifying weapon in its day that at one time helped us conquer most of France. So these Yew trees were our very armoury in the past given that the heart of the tree is unique because it has a point where it has a transition between two types of wood that turns out to make the perfect longbow with more power than anything else known in its day. Remarkably, on this score in terms of the local wood, Edwinstowe seems to have had a hand in the whole business of war and the defence of the realm, even before mining became a local phenomenon.

Some from the region would proudly claim Nottinghamshire to be the heart of England, given its position in the country and its shape as a county. Some may go even further and claim Edwinstowe to be the heart of Nottinghamshire which does seem plausible given that the whole county of Nottinghamshire has come to be identified so much with the legend of the forest there on a global scale.

Yes, Sherwood Forest is internationally known, mainly because the whole subject of Robin Hood is perhaps the most prolific and popular global people's myth of the middles ages, as it has been repeatedly depicted in film from the very first blockbuster starring Errol Flynn and his stylish tights. Just how he managed to avoid pulling threads on the brambles I will never know, but that's a celluloid hero for you. I did hear they had to have a break from filming for a week because Errol cut his finger on the bowstring. I'm not sure if that's true, but the popularity of the area is the result of the media coverage since its release in 1938 and the many films that have emerged on the same theme since then.

In truth it may surprise you to know that the same kind of myth exists in many cultures – of some outlaw who stole from the rich and gave to the poor – but it was the English version that came to be the most prolific on the global scale. When people around the world ask me where I am from all I need to say is Sherwood Forest and they know immediately where I am talking about. Some are a little surprised because they think it was all fiction, but I am soon able to set the record straight on that. Such is its fame, many people come from all over the world to visit the *Major Oak* tree and the forest, and to explore the legend which includes the medieval church with impressive spire, built in 1175 A.D., where Robin Hood and Maid Marion are believed to have been married. On the back of this legend tourist facilities have long since set up in the area, not least of which was the first *Centre Parcs* holiday village that was built in the UK, on the other side of the village to the main forest that numerous people have now visited. Fortunately for us many of the visitors stay on the park complex and enjoy the facilities, otherwise Edwinstowe and the Forest would be far busier than it is. But that is mainly because not all that come are country folk, or they don't know what a treat they are missing when they come to the area.

So that is one reason why my home village of Edwinstowe is at least a little bit famous. But as I was saying, there is another, and that is the coal mine, Thoresby Colliery that stood nearby, which until its closure in July, 2015 after 90 years of working was a major source of employment for the village and some of the other villages around and about. Though the legend of the colliery is not nearly as prolific as that of Sherwood Forest, it nevertheless has the distinction and accolade of being probably the most successful deep coal mine in Europe that there has ever been. Quite a boast, and something that the miners who worked it have every right to be eminently proud of, as much as the legend of the forest.

Thoresby Colliery was my starting place in terms of my career in mining, but this is not just about the one colliery. On a broader level it is about my experience of mining in the whole Nottinghamshire coalfield, and to some extent the whole UK national mining industry of which it was a part. I was originally signed up as a Craft Apprentice Mechanical Fitter – which simply means I was to be trained to install and maintain the machinery at the mine. However, after a year I was fortunate enough to be offered a position to train for mechanical engineering management, which meant I was immediately upgraded to the Nottinghamshire Area level and eventually destined to take control of a complete mine from a mechanical perspective. This gave me access to what was initially 15 mines, and that figure was later expanded to around 30 mines when the North and South Nottinghamshire areas combined. It also meant I entered an intensive 9 year training programme designed to give me hands on exposure to, and experience in, every aspect of the mining industry. The policy of the national industry was to make sure its managers were well versed in every aspect of the industry, so as a result I saw and experienced many aspects of mining across a whole range of mines, and this is a large part of the experience I want to pass on so the future generations of those mining communities can get an insight into what their forebears went through to establish the communities they now live in.

Mines are invariably full of big characters. Their jobs often demand physical aggression, so naturally this forms certain character traits that I have found to be common throughout the whole coal mining industry. That said, these men are all individuals, and in many ways this character development seems to bring out that individuality in ways that I think a less demanding environment may not. Of course the same is true in any institution – people are people wherever you go. But I often liken mining to war; not against an enemy, but against nature. And if you know anything about nature then you know this – she can be a very tough opponent! Of course war is about survival and freedom. About maintaining the kind of life we wish to preserve at any cost, so it is about quality of life – we battle against enemies that would otherwise dominate us and impose their ways on us. But mining is also about similar things. We all need resources; we need materials to maintain our way of life. Everything physical that we own is made of materials, and these materials come mostly from the earth.

That applies to everything from our houses, to our cars, to modern day computers and mobile phones, to everything in between. Computers require metals and materials of many kinds, including even some of the elements known as rare earth minerals. All of these have to come out of the earth we live on. There it is in the word 'mineral'. All of it must be mined. Without these minerals our quality of life will be affected, so we have to go to war just to survive – especially in this modern world. Of course coal mining is about energy – something else we are avid consumers of and another thing we really couldn't do without. Black diamonds I have heard it called. Maybe that's a bit of a romantic view, but then again when you think about it maybe we need coal more than diamonds because diamonds don't keep you warm or run your hair dryer, do they?

You will have to excuse me for occasionally showing my geeky side by waxing a bit philosophical, but it always intrigued me that the things we need to survive generally require some real talent to obtain them from the world we live in. The animals we eat generally run a lot faster than we do, or anything we grow takes so long to mature that there is the real possibility of starving to death before they are ready to provide nourishment, so we are forced to plan ahead and can't simply fly be the seat of our pants, so to speak, and do well. Mining seems to me to be just the kind of activity we are forced to engage in just to live, and we must band together and cooperate to be successful at it, especially on the scale of modern mining rather than days gone by where people would sometimes dig mines in their back garden. That was how the Black Country in the West Midlands got its name; by the coal seam that existed just a few metres below the surface so the area became pock marked with small scale mine shafts dug by those that decided to try to earn a living from it.

Mining in the modern world, like war, is a team effort; people have to rely on each other. This always creates a level of bonding, either for good or for bad. So a big part of my story is not just about the physical aspects of mining, but about the many fascinating characters I met throughout the industry. It is an insight into a culture which may be interesting for you if you are familiar with it because you will recognise much of what I write about, but also an insight for those of you that never experienced it. For you, if you are the latter, this is going to be more like a human wildlife documentary, to enlighten you on the ins-and-outs of a culture that is to some extent quite foreign to your own.

CHAPTER 2

One thing you need to understand first of all about the UK coal mines is that they were generally divided into three departments – Mining, Mechanical, and Electrical – or to be more precise Mining Engineering, Mechanical Engineering, and Electrical Engineering. This three-tiered personnel structure inevitably set the scene for a whole lot of conflict, and indeed comedy – depending on how you look at it of course. To get the ball rolling on that comedy let me tell you one way that I heard someone distinguish between the personnel in each department – and I think this must have originated from the Electrical department. It goes like this:

Electricians are people who always speak with three syllables – Electric, Resister, Thermostat, Screwdriver etc. Then there are the mechanical types; they always speak with two syllables – Hammer, Spanner, Gearbox, Toolbox etc. And finally we have the mining department who always speak with one syllable – Stick, Lamp, Boot, Nog, Chock, Face, Rock etc.

Of course for this sideswipe comment, when it emerged, it hit the mark and caused the intended outrage, but personally I have to question just who the smart guys really are. The motto of one pit wife I knew of, who admitted she had a certain common verbal condition, was 'why use two words when ten will do'. A similar principle could be assumed to apply in this case.

Remember when I said people who work as a team form some kind of bonding, whether for good or bad. Well this is a good example of the kind of comment that didn't help much on that score. One of the problems here was that power always ultimately rested with the mining department rather than the technicians so any smart-arsed comments like this always meant just one thing – retaliation. As I was part of the mechanical department this could be quite a problem. The reason was that every miner, almost without exception, fancied himself as a mechanical fitter. So if any such offensive comments were in circulation you could guarantee when the next breakdown occurred the miners would be peering over the shoulder of the mechanic ready to point out all his mistakes to prove they knew better how to do his job than he did. And so revenge would be exacted. Mechanics soon learned it is best to keep your mouth shut when the electrical department came up with something really witty like that. However, the occasional boredom of life between hectic breakdowns would sometimes get the better of the mechanic who would find himself unable to contain the banter fomenting within him and would inadvertently blurt it out. Then the stage was set for another reckoning which could range in form between anything from an episode of *Only Fools and Horses*, to a rerun of *The Good the Bad and the Ugly*.

Why didn't the electrical department feel compelled to keep their mouth shut too? Good question. I am glad you asked. Well, there is a good reason for that – which is that they were actually often the genuine smart-arses. If we had a mechanical breakdown it would most often be within the scope of understanding of the miner – e.g. 'the chain broke' (no rocket science there) – which made it kind of hard for the fitter (i.e. mechanic) to blag his way through it if the repairs went wrong. On the other hand if there was an electrical breakdown the electrician would just say – 'Oh, there's a short on the pilot interlock circuit', and that would be enough for the miner to leave him alone to fix it given that they had no idea what a pilot interlock circuit was. Sometimes, as one of the mechanical staff I felt we were the piggy in the middle. Electrician come up with the witty insults, miners take offence, and we mechanics get the backlash. Whoever said life was fair?

Now all this banter was of course what kept the whole place running and on its toes. In time everybody learned to watch their back, and indeed give as good as they got, which is a large part of the culture that would develop at a mine. It was often the only way to stem the tide of all the good humoured ridicule that would otherwise be heaped upon the victim.

Just to keep this in balance I must say, among the miners there were often some really witty characters, despite the occasional disdain of electricians and mechanics. At times these characters would 'get the chair' and give as good a comedy performance as any professional stand-up comedian I have ever seen. One such retaliatory response still makes me smile:

One of the miners told a story of the pit Manager who decided to find out how competent his staff were so he called into his offices an Overman, a Deputy, and a Mechanic. He then put them in separate rooms and gave them two ball bearings each – note: ball bearings at a pit may be an inch or more in diameter of solid steel. The manager then told them they had 15 minutes to balance one ball bearing on top of the other. When the time was up the Manager went to the room with the Overman and there were the ball bearings balanced one on top of the other. The Manager praised the Overman and asked, how did you do it? The Overman answered – well I just licked one of the balls and used surface tension to make them stick. The Manager was duly impressed. He then went to the Deputy's room and there he was with the ball bearings balanced one on top of the other. Again impressed he asked how he did it, and the Deputy said well I just rubbed one ball bearing on my clothes and used static electricity to make them stick. The Manager then went to the third room and there was the Mechanic on the floor. He said "What's the matter?" The Mechanic said, "Well, I've lost one… and I've broke the other." Of course as always this was an onslaught on the competence of the Mechanic, and the wily electricians got away scot free yet again.

This kind of banter was always in the air at a colliery and it was a kind of ongoing sport amongst the men, but as I said before, mining is a team game. If you are going to make any progress you need the help of others and so you have to cooperate with them. What that means is, between these bouts of merciless banter there would also be a fair amount of appeasement where those that were insulted yesterday or last week are now needed to accomplish a task, so the offenders would have to 'butter them up' again to get them back on side. To live with this Jekyll and Hyde treatment and survive, everyone needed to develop a nice thick rhino hide, and a fairly versatile sense of humour. That would mean plenty of forgive and forget, which is always a great character building exercise for anybody, and not least seasoned miners.

Sometimes, I observed, the use of the insults themselves would be strategic. For example the mechanical department often needed the help of the mining department to dig out some machinery that was covered in debris before they could work on it. Naturally to get the help the mechanical department manager would speak nicely to the mining department to ask for help. But I did see some occasions when, for example one time a mechanical manager asked the mining department to send him three 'rock apes' to do the digging. Of course no self-respecting miner would respond to such a title so the job would not get done that day. This seemed like bad management and counter-productive. However what transpired was that the mechanical department didn't have the staff for the job that day but didn't want to admit it because that would seem to the bosses like bad management. Naturally the alternative was to insult the miners so they refused to turn up, then they could be blamed for the delay. In the end I had to give credit to the cunning strategy of the mechanical shift managers on this occasion and appreciate the comedy value of it all.

CHAPTER 3

Sometimes, when you go down a pit you see sights that are only ever likely to recur in your worst nightmares. On one such occasion I visited a coalface where the temperature was 43 C (110 F). At those temperatures the men would strip down to the bare minimum clothing. One sight I will never forget is meeting a huge miner down a dark roadway. He was wearing all the obligatory gear of helmet, lamp, socks, boots and kneepads, and the only other item of clothing was his grey pit issue Y-front underpants. He was dirty of course, but this guy had a huge beer belly, bald, no teeth, and was chewing a twist of tobacco, occasionally spitting it into the darkness with the stains of tobacco spit running down his chest and his belly. It was the closest I have seen to Jabba the Hut in real life.

On very few occasions I have known a party of women or girls visit a coalface. This is a very rare thing, but it did occasionally happen. On this particular face I was rather fearful for them of the sights they may encounter, though I was hoping the Deputies would make the men put all their full gear back on before the girls arrived. As it happened the men on the coal face got wind of the perfume the girls were wearing as they were entering through the intake air roadway, which may run for miles, and as a joke they started howling over the Tannoy speaker system. The girls heard it over the speaker system and got scared and refused to go any further so their guides had to lead them all back, having already spent considerable efforts bolstering their courage to embolden them to make the trip. I believe the men were reprimanded by the management for their 'ungentlemanly behaviour' but to be quite honest I was relieved they never made it, though I guess they must have had a sleepless night or two thinking that experience over – sometimes the unseen is scarier than the seen. Now I wouldn't want to suggest men turn into werewolves or anything when they work on a coalface, but I have to say there is something of the roughness of that environment that seems to get into them as soon as they descend the mine shaft. After all they do descend in what we call a 'cage'; often one that has multiple decks and 50 men on each deck so there may be as many as 120 or more men descending in one go. In many cases I would meet the same men on the streets of the local villages and hardly recognise them, they just seemed like normal people, but here at the mine they were readying themselves for yet another battle, so the mood invariably changed.

There was an unspoken protocol when descending the mine in the cage of lights out, and silence. You would simply feel the sensation of slight weightlessness as the cage accelerated and you were dropped into blackness, together often with the bodies of men crushing around you. There was a surreal sense to it that has to be experienced to be appreciated. One of the lasting memories I had from Thoresby Colliery was of a miner that would break the protocol and sing at the top of his voice as we descended the mine. His singing was superb – he definitely had the X-Factor, even though this was long before the show. His voice would echo in the mine shaft in a unique and ghostly way that is difficult to forget.

Mineshafts can be scary places. The blacksmiths at the mine were always the ones charged with maintaining the shaft, and as with all departments I had to spend some time with them. As you move further north and east in Nottinghamshire the coal seams get deeper. There are actually more than 200 coal seams under the Nottinghamshire area. Many of them are just a few inches in height and so not workable, but the ones we worked were normally between about 4.5 feet and 8 feet in height. The highest seam I ever saw mined was about 10 feet high at another Nottinghamshire Colliery. The shaft at Thoresby was about 700m deep. To the east was another mine I worked at for some years called Bevercotes Colliery. This was even deeper; in fact the deepest we had at 1000m (i.e. 1 km straight down).

There is a story of a big blunder with Bevercotes Colliery when they first sank the pit. This was much later than all the other mines in the area in the early 1960s. Usually many bore holes would be drilled to prove the coal seams in the area before sinking (digging) a shaft because sinking is very (very) expensive. The shaft has to pass through water bearing strata so to handle that the way Bevercotes accomplished it was to freeze the ground around the shaft by drilling holes and then pumping refrigerant down. That would freeze the water and the sinkers would dig through the frozen ground. Then once through the water bearing strata the shaft would be lined with 'tubbing', which looked like the inside of a huge barrel. That would hold the water back so they could then thaw it without the whole seam of water emptying into the mine and flooding it. As I said, there was a big blunder. Very few exploratory holes had been drilled before sinking the mine. The results were so good they didn't even drill a hole where the shaft was planned to be and they quickly approved the mine to be sunk. When the shaft got to the level where the coal was known to be at about 700m deep it simply wasn't there. In panic they carried on sinking to a deeper level of 1000m to get a lower coal seam of a good height but inferior quality. However what they didn't realise was that when they reached the higher seam level they had passed through what we call a washout. This is where an ancient river had run and swept the coal away for the width of the river. The truth was the seam was there but not in the exact spot where they had sunk the shaft. It was simply bad luck. The lower seam that Bevercotes worked was a lower coal quality, and thus worth less, though it was ideal for power stations. But it is always a problem to try to mine a higher seam after a lower one because the subsidence from the lower seam removal will in some measure break up the higher seam. As I said – it was a big expensive blunder, though Bevercotes Colliery did become a viable colliery for many years, even if not profitable.

To be fair to Bevercotes the fact it was sunk much later than other mines really made it impossible to be profitable. Sinking a mine and installing it became an immensely expensive exercise so when the profit margins on coal were tight, or non-existent, profitability was out of the question. Over time mining engineering installations got ridiculously expensive, which may be partly a result of it becoming a nationalised industry; that meant its owner, the government, were always known to have the money to subsidise it so prices always went up. I once visited an even later new mine installation; Asforby in the Belvoir Vale in Leicestershire – designated to be a 'superpit'. The installation was budgeted to cost £1 billion and after opening in 1991 it closed in 1997 – a massive waste of money. The chances of profitability of such a mine were nil and it really was an ill-conceived venture from the start despite the fact there are coal reserves down there.

Mines in Nottinghamshire could be as deep as a kilometre, and the workings could extend out for as much as 10 miles (16 km). At these distances travel times would be significant and transport would be essential. As a Mechanical Shift Charge engineering manager my duties often required me to deploy men, who would catch the transport to the workings they were sent to, and I would follow when I had deployed them all, usually travelling to some mechanical trouble spot in the mine that needed some direction. Often my deployment duties would delay me which would mean I missed the transport. The consequence of that could be a walk of 7 miles through pitch black tunnels that were sometimes slowly closing up badly under the weight that was pressing down on them. The solitary nature of this kind of blackness and remoteness has to be experienced to be appreciated. Consider also that in one mine I worked at – Mansfield Crown Farm Colliery, there were five simultaneously active seams being worked, each at different levels. That would mean a real rabbit warren of tunnels that often crossed over each other. Learning the layout of such a mine would be a challenge in itself. Then if you were caught out and forced to go on one of these very long treks to a trouble spot, sometimes as you walked doubts would develop in your mind that you were going the right way. It is scary how such a thought can play on your mind over a 7 mile trek in pitch black darkness to the point where you even doubt the things you were certain of when you set off. Given that I worked at many mines, the propensity to get confused on the layout was very real, especially given that underground roadways often look very similar to each other. Imagine the relief I felt when finally coming to the end of the tunnel and arriving at my intended destination. Of course such relief would have to be carefully concealed from the men. Any weakness shown would become a point of gossip that would rapidly travel to all corners of the pit if it got out, and there was always a significant chance that someone of a certain disposition would interpret your uncertainties as an opportunity for psychological sport, just to break up the boredom which would inevitably accompany the miners in a breakdown situation. I will probably never know just what level of fear some of my men were really concealing in their day to day lives working at a coal mine.

There were many cases I became aware of where a man had had a bad accident, or had seen others have such an accident. Like war, it had the capacity to traumatise those that experienced it. There were some cases, after such an event, where men became desperate to get back to the surface, and once out of the mine were unable to ever enter it again. I have even known this to happen with men for no apparent reason whatsoever. Something in them simply snapped and after that wild horses couldn't drag them back down the mine. These cases were usually deployed thereafter to the pit top as that was clearly the only option for them. For them the lower surface wages were a small price to pay in contrast to the idea of going down the confined spaces of a mine again.

CHAPTER 4

One of the mining regulations stated there has to be a means of emergency evacuation for miners from the mine in case the winding gear broke down. The regulations demanded this emergency method would have to be tested every two years. It consisted of a lorry turning up to the mine with a huge drum of thick wire rope on the back. The lorry would anchor to the floor near the shaft and the rope would be threaded over a pulley in the shaft headgear. They then attached a huge bucket, loaded three men, and lifted the bucket to dangle it over the shaft. This was scary as it was over a drop of 1 km straight down. I was training at the time but I figured you only live once and so volunteered for the ride. There were three of us in the bucket; the deputy engineer, a blacksmith, and myself. The lorry winch picked us up and we swung over the shaft. We were then gradually lowered down the full kilometre of the shaft with the intention of landing on top of the cage that was normally used for access but now parked at pit bottom. The deputy engineer had a radio with which to communicate with the lorry and his plan was to shout 'stop' when we got near to the cage, and then to very slowly travel down again and land squarely in a stepped recess on top of the cage. However, when we got close to the cage and the deputy engineer shouted 'STOP', the response was delayed. That made us travel too far and the bottom of our bucket caught the edge of the recess, tipping the bucket as it did. Then before the bucket tipped us out it slid into the recess. At that moment we had to check our hearts were still beating. After a few moments of shock the rocking bucket came to rest so we felt we had been lucky and got away with it. Then, about a minute later the bucket began to violently rock again. The deputy engineer starting panicking and shouting to the other two of us to stop rocking the bucket, but all we could do was to say it wasn't us; we weren't doing it. We then realised what was happening. The original mistake had set off a vibration wave in the rope, like a 1 kilometre long guitar string, and that wave was taking a whole minute to travel to the surface and back to us again. So about every minute we got a decreasing vibration wave hit us, like a seismic wave of an earthquake that would rock the bucket again. Eventually it stopped, but it was one of those heart stopping experiences you sometimes get in mining where something serious nearly did go wrong.

The mine shaft is often the most precarious place in a mine. There is a lot that can go wrong if you are not careful. It was the blacksmiths at a mine that would take most of the responsibilities for the maintenance of these shafts. These individuals tended to be a particular kind of rough, tough character. Not quite your usual mechanical fitter types, but ones that aspired to that kind of job but were often less qualified than the mechanical fitters. As always every man is an individual and there were men amongst them you would trust with your life. On the other hand I was aware of some really rough characters, who, if they took a dislike to you were best avoided. I remember at least one place I worked where one of the blacksmiths turned out to be a criminal who the police were pursuing. Though we or his workmates didn't know about his crimes, when they finally closed in on him he chose his own way out by committing suicide. His crimes included some very heinous activities found in witchcraft or Satanism and the like. It is all I am prepared to say about that case, and I probably only know very little of the truth, but my point is, despite most miners being people you can absolutely trust, and do trust on a regular basis, there were nevertheless some that were a real rotten apple and you had to be aware of those risks. Especially where you intended to follow such a character into the most dangerous place imaginable at the pit; the mine shaft.

There would usually be two mine shafts at a pit – one the air intake, and the other the air outlet, also known as the 'return'. The return shaft would be very hot, but the intake shaft could be freezing, especially in winter where temperatures in the shaft could reach minus 30 Celsius. On occasions I saw blacksmiths walking the plank in the shaft to reach the shaft wall for some maintenance purpose. There were gutters to fix and sometimes brickwork to repair. To reach the wall they would ride on top of the cage and take a long plank. Two of them would then sit on the end of the plank while the other walked out on the limb with the open mine shaft below them. Of course the regulations demand a harness, but there were times, being the characters they were, where these men would 'bend the rules'. If their act was found out by the management it would have meant the sack for certain, but you still see them take risks like this at times, nevertheless. On one occasion I heard of blacksmiths that were called out to a breakdown where the cage was stuck in the guiders in the mine shaft near the pit top. These guys decided to get to the cage by running and leaping over the shaft and grabbing one of the winding ropes, then sliding down the rope onto the cage. On this occasion the act was reported and the men were in fact sacked. Why did they do it? Sometimes this was foolish nonchalance having spent a great deal of time working with the dangers in the shaft. After all the same was true of the steel monkeys that built the huge sky scrapers like the Empire State Building, New York. At other times I observed the motive was something else. A blacksmith had a certain unique street credibility as a rough, tough dude. To take such risks in the shaft would inevitably be talked about, which of course would really enhance their street credibility. It was something to talk about in the welfare over a pint that evening after the shift. Sometimes these motivators are hard to discourage at a mine and there can be a certain competition going on for credibility like this.

CHAPTER 5

It has been observed in war that even where men are under constant threat of death from enemy fire, there is a banter and jollity that just seems to carry on regardless. Tolstoy's famous book War and Peace includes much of this kind of observation in the war on the Russian front against the Napoleonic forces. One occasion like this at the pit sticks in my mind with the blacksmiths. A new apprentice blacksmith had joined them and was due to head down the shaft on top of the cage for the first time. Of course he was a little nervous at the prospect, but a brave lad and willing to go to prove himself to the men. The blacksmiths then began to talk amongst themselves with him listening on. They were debating who was going to fight off the shaft bats. Of course this apprentice had never been told there were bats in the shaft, or that there was any need to defend yourself against them. Eventually they decided the new apprentice would be the one to defend them from the bats while they did the work, so they armed him with a stick. He then had to wait for a couple of hours for the maintenance window where he had time to think about it, not realising he was under the close and gleeful observation of his older workmates. When the time came he was then marched off with them to the shaft, stick at the ready. Of course he would pass the test if he got all the way to the shaft without bottling, which he did, where he would discover there weren't in fact any bats to fight. But he would be hailed a hero for accepting the job and soon accepted as a fully initiated blacksmith after his trial. Of course it didn't take long before that kind of naivety wore off so the men made the most of it while the recruit was still green and gullible, even though they would usually treat their apprentices with a great deal of affection, all carefully concealed behind a tough exterior of course.

Often at a mine there are unbelievably risky jobs to be done. On one occasion at Bevercotes while I was in management training a mechanical fitter was deployed to shin out on a girder over the main underground coal bunker at the mine to drill holes in a girder ready for mounting some machine on it at the weekend. This bunker was where all the coal that had been won would be stored underground ready for extraction and the bunker was like another shaft, about 100 metres deep, that would fill with coal and rock. His job was to drill holes for machinery to be mounted on the girder above it when the mine was shut down at the next weekend. The problem was there was no way the coal flow could be stopped to allow this job to be done – that would mean the whole pit would stand still at great expense. It had to be done while the mine was running at full tilt. I had some ideas on how to operate the drill in such a difficult environment and so volunteered to go. Any job that was out of the ordinary was a chance for real experience, so I often preferred to get involved in these jobs, and the men were always thankful for the extra hand. When I got to the job it was like hell itself. A boiling cauldron of coal dust descending into sheer murky blackness below where the roar of coal pouring into the bunker could be heard. To fall in would mean certain death. We had our harnesses, and we stuck to the rules. But it was a job I will always remember. Again it was one of those jobs that had a level of street credibility to it with the men, and that kind of job was always a help for a training engineering manager like myself that was prepared to do it. In the end we had to command respect from these men to get the work done, so this strategy of facing the worst jobs head-on did pay dividends on many occasions. This was perhaps the limit I was prepared to go to, but there were men who were my friends that went much further. Often the jobs were so difficult and specialised that contractors were employed to do them. These were men that had proved their stripes and were ready for the very worst of the worst. I remember one such job where the men, including a personal friend, were employed to dig a shaft, but on this occasion it was underground and it had to be dug upwards, not downward. The hazards of cutting away rock above you with a considerable drop below is unbelievably dangerous. Therefore the men would be paid handsomely for the work. When my friend and his team completed the job there was a celebration and awards to commemorate what they had achieved, much like in war. But sadly on the evening of the celebration, despite having been no accidents on this job, his best friend and colleague had an accident and fell down the shaft to his death. These men are real comrades and they develop an incredible bond when they risk their lives together like this. The loss of a friend like that was a devastating thing for them, but they inevitably showed the same bravado and buried their feelings despite the fact I knew personally how much grief my friend was going through over the loss.

A pit top is often a much more pleasant place to work than underground, though even here there is an ongoing battle with the environment, and sometimes the added problem of atrocious weather which is one benefit of going underground – you escape the weather. The payoff is you get to enjoy the sunshine when the weather is nice, but during my training years I often found myself working on the pit top on machinery when it was snowing or there was snow on the ground.

One of the biggest challenges of installing mining machinery is stripping it down to a size that will fit down the mine shaft and through the roadways. I liken this to the old pub competitions of smashing up an old piano and shoving it all through a toilet seat. The first one to get the whole piano through wins. Passing a piano is quite an eye watering practice, but installing machinery in a mine is worse because not only do you have to strip it down to small pieces, you have to transport it for miles, and then build it up again in some very confined spaces.

During one of these installations there was an occasion that won me a great deal of that street credibility I was talking about. Not intentionally I might add, but one of those things that just happened in my favour. At this time I was in charge of a shift at a mine and so commanding the respect of the men was an ongoing issue. The incident happened on a coalface we were installing and it required one man to hold a long steel shaft/pin about 60mm in diameter and another to hit it with a sledge hammer. I volunteered to hold the pin. As it happens a mining Undermanager happened to grab the sledge hammer to show his willingness to have a go. Not the normal kind of person for a job like this as he was a manager, he was from the mining department, and he was fairly young, but I felt I had to respect his enthusiasm. He swung the hammer at the pin I was holding, and yes, you guessed it, he missed. The sledge hammer travelled down the side of the pin and hit me on the hands. At this point you may be wincing and wondering how I managed to type this book. However, what happened was my hands slid down the bar and as I was gripping it tightly friction gradually braked the blow to a standstill. Did it hurt? Not at all. You see a big hammer doesn't really travel that fast. It would only cause real harm if my hand was between it and a hard place. Instead the friction on the bar slowly braked it to a standstill with no damage to me whatsoever. Nevertheless there were quite a few men watching and they winced like you did. I then realised I was safe, even from this guy, so I replaced my hands on the pin and said 'try again'. This drew some astonishment from those watching. The Undermanager turned white, but managed to hold himself together and followed my instruction, this time making sure he hit the target for the next three blows. That incident was talked about throughout the pit and gave me a bit of a superman status for a while – but it was all really simple mechanical principles.

There was one other incident during the same period that also really helped me get some respect, and get a handle on the men I was managing. It came when I had to withdraw some men from working underground to work on some machinery on the pit top. It was a snowy day and these men were used to working in heat underground – it is hot down there even on snowy days. One thing often not realised is that if you get half a metre below the surface of the ground it is unaffected by the surface temperature. From there the temperature increases by about 1 C for every 40 metres down, so a mine of 1 km depth has a considerable temperature increase in the rock strata. This is known as the geothermal gradient. The nearer you get to the molten core of the earth, the hotter it is. In places like South Africa there are gold mines that are so deep the managers that go there from climates like the UK can only stand the heat for a couple of hours, even though the local natives would work in it all day. In our mines the initial air intake is at the surface temperature but this geothermal heat soon warms it up. Heat is then also added my men and machinery so temperatures can be like a beach in Ibiza, as the men would describe it. Anyway, as I was saying, I deployed men to the surface, but they had a huge moan about the weather and wanted to go back to Ibiza, which they couldn't – the job had to be done. As a compromise I negotiated the use of the surface workshop that was really for the surface fitters, not the underground fitters. So far so good. They nearly finished the job. By nearly I mean the one thing they didn't do is clean up the mess they made. Machines get covered in muck, so all this muck was on the floor in the fitting shop. Part of the job would be to clean it up, but unfortunately a colleague of mine on another shift decided to redeploy them before they had a chance to do the clean-up. This let them off the hook and I was mad about it, but not half as mad as Mack, the surface fitting shop foreman. The muck stayed for days, and the foreman refused to touch it, giving me grief every day. I demanded the men return and finish the job. In the end I picked up a yard brush and shovel myself and cleaned it up. I then called in all underground personnel involved and gave the warranted rollicking. Though others would have stood their ground on principle, I made it understood this was a once only. Nevertheless it seemed to have a good effect for me because the men realised I was willing to do the dirty jobs too if needed to cover their backs and keep the job rolling. It never happened again and we got onto a new understanding that the clean-up was and is part of the job in every case. I came from a mine where this was already understood (Thoresby), but not all mines were so professional and it seems this was a new lesson for them.

CHAPTER 6

I have a background of being raised in a mining village. Though my father was not a miner, both of my grandfathers were, so both of my parents came from mining familics. The grandfather on my mother's side was also an Overman at Thoresby Colliery, the local mine. The position of Overman is as high as a working man could normally expect to rise in the pit, though there were notable exceptions. There are usually several Overmen that cover the different general areas of the pit. Above them in respective order are the Undermanager/s, the Deputy Manager, and the general pit Manager, all of whom are usually trained from the beginning to be higher level managers. Below them are a whole slew of Deputies, of which there may be many. These are the officials required by law, who invariably used to be workers, and they effectively oversee every active place in the mine, and the inactive ones too. All of these mining officials belong to the mining department. Electrical and Mechanical departments have their own structure but in the UK mines both of these technical departments answered to the mining department. Generally these mining officials had a great deal of pride in their position, whatever they were, and there was a kind of badge of honour that marked them out as an official, as opposed to a worker. This was the famous Davey Lamp. A manager or official in the mining department would always carry a Davey Lamp. This was not for light; they had an electric battery lamp for that, but it was a lamp designed to test for the presence of methane gas. The strange thing about this was that we had instruments called methanometers that would read the methane levels at the press of a button. They were much simpler to use and they didn't involve the hazard of carrying an enclosed naked flame as the Davey

Lamps did. So why did they still carry the lamps? This is where the mining culture really manifests itself. First the Davey Lamp was like a badge that identified an official, and so demanded respect. Secondly the mining regulations demanded that no-one carrying a lamp could do any work (at least without taking specific precautions), so a lamp was a way of making perfectly clear that you were not a manual labourer but were there to command and oversee others as they do the work.

I always found the deputies were great characters at the pit. Again all individuals of course, but generally seasoned characters that all had their own way of managing the men that worked under them. Generally there would be an ongoing personality battle between the deputies and the men. All this was played out like a big game that was often quite amusing for onlookers like myself. Of course it was the men themselves that were exerting all the effort and aggression that got the job done, so they were really interesting characters too. Many of them had an issue with anybody having any authority over them, but were often caught between a rock and a hard place with the wives they were trying to keep happy back at home. In other words they needed the job and so they had to toe the line, or else; given that the pit wives were actually the people with the real power. In truth pit wives could be truly formidable when you saw them dominating the domestic scene. Rebelling against a Deputy would be a piece of cake compared to that. Of course there were always some that were out-and-out rebels, but it was the wily Deputies that had the job of handling them. Generally we as technical staff would work through the Deputies if we needed any help or cooperation from the miners, but we inevitably clashed with them sometimes. Much of the time the view the men had of us was a little bit like it was for the Deputies – there was a certain disdain. They often assumed we thought ourselves better than them as technicians and so at times we had to deal with the backlash that came from that.

One of my first learning experiences on what a real miner can be like came one day when a huge miner crawled out from the coalface into the roadway, saw my water bottle and said to me 'give us a drink of watter youth'. At this time I was new to the whole thing and very green. Who was I to deny him, especially given the size of the guy? As he began glugging down my precious water I could see in the clear plastic bottle the brown stains and pieces of chewing tobacco he was chewing floating all through the whole bottle. I realised later this was just a huge deliberate joke for the miners on the face there so I quickly wised up to their antics, but for this day I can tell you I was pretty thirsty by the time I got back to the pit surface again.

As I said earlier, my grandfather on my mother's side was a miner and an Overman at Thoresby Colliery, from the village I lived in. He retired when I was very young and so spent a great deal of time helping to raise me and my brothers. His name was Eric Swanwick. He, like the rest, was a real individual who made his way to the top of the ladder through sheer hard graft. Before mining he had worked in Nottingham at a gun factory. Having been born in 1901 this put him working there in his early teens and during WWI. My grandmother once shared with me an incredible story from this time. She was at Nottingham's Victoria train station when suddenly everything stopped and became still. After half an hour of this silence she saw a German Zeppelin fly over looking for the gun factory where my grandfather worked, preparing to bomb it. That as we know was the beginning of an awesome century of war where aerial warfare was a whole new thing. Hearing of its beginning from someone who witnessed it first hand was an amazing thing for me. Later my grandfather decided to move to the mines for the better wages, but I know from what he told me it turned out to be an incredibly tough life choice he made back then. It also shortened his life. The doctors reckoned apart from his lungs he would have lasted at least another ten years.

In my grandfather's day the work of a miner was incredibly manual. Machinery arrived gradually over time but in his day a large part of the work was using explosives and then pick and shovel. At its height during Eric's time the UK mines employed more than a million men. In my day that was down to around 250,000 which was mainly due to mechanisation. In the end my grandfather died of pneumoconiosis, the coal miner's lung disease. It seemed a difficult and tragic death, but he was nearly eighty by then. I was aged about 22 at the time of his death. As a child I came to love these grandparents dearly. Apart from my mother, they were perhaps the adults I spent most quality time with as Eric's retirement from the mine made possible.

I didn't realise it as a child but Eric's management style at the pit was to always live on the edge of real grumpy outburst. He was hard to please, and he made you try hard to please him. Sometimes as a child that would spill over into our relationship where he would tell me something and I would ask the question 'why Grandad?' This kind of question was always ok with my mother, but with my grandad you always got a startled response, like I had done something wrong. His back would straighten like he was bracing to react. Then I would see the reflex action subside as it occurred to him he was speaking to his grandson and not the Deputies as he was accustomed to. He would then think carefully for a moment, as if pondering my question, and then relax and give me an answer. I just thought it was his way, and this was how grandads were. I was too young to know any different back then. But underneath his ingrained grumpiness was a man with a very soft and loving heart that would have done anything for us. He still had his pride, and that way of demanding respect he had learned managing rough characters in the mine was ingrained. It all came from a lifetime where he learned to survive in an incredibly tough environment. Like the rest, he did it for his family and I owe him a huge debt of gratitude for that.

One memory I have of him as a growing boy was his advice to me about life and career – 'never smoke, and never work at the pit'. Maybe that was said to protect my lungs as the disease was now gripping him, or maybe it was his reflection on an incredibly hard life he would like to spare me from. I don't know, but I fully intended to take his advice. As a result I never smoked. I never even had a drag on a cigarette. In some ways I think I was rebelling against my friends that were trying to pressure me to do it. Looking back I think there was something in my genes that always made me push back against those kinds of forces, but I also think the advice of my grandad on his deathbed made me think twice. That said, of course I did end up in the mines against his advice. In truth I initially resisted that idea and at school whereas I lived with kids who assumed they were destined for the pit, like their parents, and so declined to work at their studies, I had the idea I was destined for something else and so after a slow academic start I made up lost ground. After all, my father was not a miner. Nor indeed was my uncle Barry, the only sibling of my mother and son of Eric, my grandad. Clearly Grandad had given Barry the same advice he gave me – don't work at the pit. He had gone to college and become qualified as an engineer. He then went on to design some highly innovative inventions in the heady days of British

Aerospace after WW2, such as a gyroscope to control the flight of rockets. At his death he had a record of 17 patents filed in his name.

CHAPTER 7

My Dad also became qualified as an Engineer and then in time became a leading national stress analysis engineer working initially for Rolls Royce in Derby and then Hucknall when I was a kid. Then, when I was aged 11, he took redundancy when Rolls Royce nearly folded due to technical design blunders, but was rescued by the government, and he used his redundancy pay out and savings to build a house for our growing family two miles away in Ollerton. I returned to Edwinstowe 8 years later after I was married to live in the house my grandad had occupied on the mining estate, and in which my mother grew up, but for my adolescent years the new house known as Shalom in Ollerton was to be my new home. Shalom means peace, but with a family of our size you would perhaps expect that to be a contradiction. In truth it was a real place of peace and idyllic in many ways, despite many of the usual stresses and strains of family life. I am in fact the second of nine children, which was an unusually large family for my day, but what is more unusual is that there were five boys first, followed by four girls last – Craig, Trevor (Me), John, Clive, Ralph, Rachel, Sharon, Vivienne and Joy. When the house was completed it was actually a bungalow, but a very big one set on a quarter of an acre of land, with a river/stream running at the bottom of the garden and an incredible view across fields to the forest further in the distance. Every sunny evening would give us an amazing sunset over the forest through panoramic windows to the lounge. When the house building began there were six of us – Rachel, the first girl, had just been born – so the new house was needed.

This house building experience was probably my first serious exposure to engineering beyond my much loved toy Lego and Mechano sets. I spent two years with my Dad on the project from age 11 to 13, which was like slave labour because my every spare moment for those two years was devoted to the cause. None of it was forced labour though I may add; I volunteered for the job, but it was a hard, hard, hard initiation to a working life for an 11 year old. After knocking down most of the old barn that stood on the land I had three months of continuous brick cleaning so the bricks could be reused. That was gruelling to say the least. The next job was better though. We had bought a pile of left over stone from a merchant for £10. I spent a month or so splitting them open to expose the colours so we could build a magnificent chimney.

As you will realise from TV programmes like Grand Designs, no project like this ever goes completely to plan, and many of them go way over budget. Add to that the fact that in the late seventies the bank base rates shot up into double figures even reaching over 15% at its peak, then you realise why we entered a new phase of life where money was incredibly tight. We moved into the house, which was complete to a liveable standard, but my Dad was forced to take contracts that meant he worked away from home all week on projects like the Space Shuttle Development in Bristol, or defence systems in Stevenage or Hemel Hempstead, or British Rail in Bristol, and he did this until he retired. From that time on money was always tight, and the family was still growing. That said, we were fed like kings, such were the standards of my incredibly hard working and devoted mother. But things like fashion and luxury possessions became a thing of the past.

Under the financial pressures of this time my Dad drove old decrepit cars. At one point the AA brought him home so many times he was on first name terms with the rescue men and there was a rumour they were going to pay him to join the RAC. Then one day he nearly ran out of options with another failing car. He had a spare car, just as old and decrepit, and a scrap car he had acquired with the idea to cannibalise it and make the backup failing car good – at least for a while. The one thing he had not worked out was how to get the time to work on it. In that situation, when I was aged 13, he turned to me and gave me the challenge of my life – to switch the engine from the scrap car to the failing car – and to do it without his help. I had a little experience of motorbikes at this stage that I had been given by a friend, but nothing more. I didn't know what any part of the car was under the bonnet, and there was no internet like there is today for information and guidance. I agreed to do what I could. My younger brother and I spent many hours that week and burned the midnight oil – which was an omen for things to come. I thought the matter over of how to do the job and I had an epiphany when I realised if I detached everything connected to the engine then it would come out, even if I didn't know what those things were. One of the gobsmacking, astounding, unbelievable moments of my life was when, having installed the engine, it actually started. As a 13 year old it was hard to believe, but here began my life as an engineer, and I loved it, even though it was really hard work. That said, like the house building there were times when we got really tired and weary – I had the help of my little brother, Clive, who quite frankly proved to be a budding genius with anything practical and that helped a lot. That tiredness sometimes led to despair as we tried our best to keep the family mobile, but what an incredible training ground this was for my future career as an engineer.

One memory I have from a few years into this was when someone sold us a 3.5 litre Rover V8 for £10, but the engine had warped cylinder heads and needed repairs. The repairs meant removing the cylinder heads and getting them skimmed at a workshop. The workshop we had to get to was in Nottingham 20 miles away, and we had no transport while Dad was away. There are two of these cylinder heads on the V8 engine and they are long heavy beasts; just about manageable to lift and carry for one person. Clive and I were both in different colleges in Nottingham at the time so we decided to take one each on the bus with us and each get it to the workshop there at the earliest opportunity. To spice it up we made a bet on who would be the first to get it to the workshop. There was only a Mars Bar at stake, but it was also a matter of pride. I got out of class early as soon as I could, with both classmates and lecturers bemused at the huge hunk of car engine I was lugging around with me. As I rounded the Ice Stadium in Nottingham, carrying this huge chunk of metal, thinking I had fooled Clive into thinking I couldn't get there until lunch time, there he suddenly appeared 50 yards ahead of me with his huge chunk of engine in tow, having pulled the same decoy trick I had tried to level at him. I paid my debt but still don't admit to losing, just that I came second on this occasion. Those were tough years but an incredible learning curve. We swapped engines and gearboxes frequently, we welded bodies and exhausts, we reconditioned engines, we raided scrapyards, and we survived. At one point we reached 11 cars or vans in the front yard, and people began to ask if we were running a scrapyard. I guess we were. But in all of this we sometimes got so fed up working on those old decrepit vehicles we decided we needed time out to do something of our own, and that is how our famous legendary go-kart was born.

As the saying goes 'while the cat's away the mice will play'. I guess there was something of that kind of mentality in us boys when our Dad went off to work all week. Had he been around I doubt the go-kart project would have reached first base, but given any chance at all of doing something like that, believe me it was a young lad's dream and we were going to take it. Some described the finished article as a Monster, a Monolith, and Kartzilla. In our minds that was all to the good. Had that guy Heath Robinson seen it I'm guessing he would have thought it rather neat.

The problem was we had zero budget and just a whole lot of scrap to work with. We had to be innovative and imaginative and use what we had available. The first thing we did was to rob the rear axle from one of the scrap cars. Then we needed a frame. The house that we built was originally a huge barn. We knocked most of it down at the beginning of the build but some of it was (and is) the original walls of the buildings. From the parts of the building we knocked down there was a huge pile of wooden beams. We decided to make the kart frame from these and make use of some of the spare scaffolding poles that were left from the build. We literally nailed the frame together to house the differential and the two front wheels. We took seats, engine and gearbox from another car. We then connected the gearbox directly to the rear wheel drive differential, cutting out the original prop shaft and making a short go-kart like vehicle. We installed the engine. Then I installed the wiring by stripping it from one of the cars and replicating the ignition circuit on the go-kart, nailing all the components to the frame. We installed the battery, and held our breath. We turned the key. The engine turned over but it didn't start. There was no spark to the spark plugs. At this point the project hit an intellectual block. Why no spark? All the components were there. For a week there was no answer and we thought the project was going to fail. Then, as I pondered the problem, I had another epiphany. It is these moments in life when you learn the most I can tell you. I had earthed all the electrics onto the wooden frame. Ah! Oops! I soon managed to run an earth wire around the vehicle and earthed all the components onto it. Finally a spark! Then, as we were about to test the monster, Dad returned home driving his current old cronk up the dirt road driveway next to us.

The project had taken many weeks but so far Dad had turned a blind eye to it thinking it was going to fail, hoping we would get back to mending his cronky old cars. We had solved many problems to get to this stage, including one that the steering worked opposite to what you expect – when you turned the wheel left it went right. It was the weirdest thing to try to drive it as we did for a while under push power; your brain needed a complete rewire to do it. That problem was easily rectified by removing a lever from its splines on the steering mechanism and rotating it by 180 degrees. When my Dad came home and heard us turning over the engine trying to start it the reality suddenly seemed to dawn on him that it might just succeed. It was then the mood changed and he started inventing all the reasons he could think of as to why the project was doomed to failure. I think he had anticipated the truth; that we were on the verge of killing ourselves with the power of a 1500cc engine in a Heath Robinson go-kart that defined the very antithesis of an MOT. To his relief we then hit another setback. When we put the gearbox in first gear and turned the starter motor over the kart shot backwards – weird! Then we put the gearbox in reverse and turned it over and the kart shot forwards. Like the wiring issue, this was another mind boggler and again the project stood still while we thought about the problem. How could the gears possibly be reversed? We couldn't see how it was possible. Was the engine turning over backwards? But how? Then once again, after long sessions of mental gymnastics trying to solve the problem, I had another epiphany. We had nailed the rear axle in upside down. Once again Ah! And Oops! Only this time it was a much bigger problem. The trouble was the differential was nailed tightly into the frame and to get it out would destroy the whole kart. We hadn't reckoned on ever having to remove it.

To say Dad was relieved was an understatement, but there was still the nightmare scenario that we would get the engine going and then race around the fields going forwards using the reverse gear. Or worse still race around backwards at very high speed using the four forward gears that were now acting in reverse. I reckoned our kart had the capacity to beat any known vehicle in reverse so there were records to be set and glory to be won. At this point Dad randomly and unexplainably decided he wanted to park his car in the garage. That meant evicting the go-kart. We thought it was strange because he never parked his car in the garage. Nevertheless he was very insistent, so we complied and removed the kart, but that evening his strategy became clear. There was a heavy downpour of rain which filled the engine with water and it quickly rusted up. That scuppered the cornfield speed record attempt in reverse of course, but it still left us with a really cool push powered go-kart that lasted quite a few years and gave us lots of fun – far better than the pram wheel trolleys we had risked our lives on in the past.

The final demise of the kart came after a few years when Ralph, my little brother who was desperate to become a driver, took his chance and pushed it up a steep hill near the house all on his own when no one was watching, and then rode it down the hill, removing most of the paint from the side of a neighbour's car. The police were called and Ralph was given the stern face, but in truth the policemen were hugely impressed with the beast and couldn't help laughing about it given that their complaint said a car had been scraped by a trolley. It was then Dad gave Ralph the wood saw and made him do the dirty deed that ended an epic season and the best learning curve I ever had in my engineering history. In truth I made many mistakes on this project, but the learning curve was invaluable, not just for me, but also to the NCB because most budding engineers who enter service in the coal industry tend to make their early mistakes at the cost of the industry, whereas I was already quite seasoned in these things before I even got there.

Of course when I was born and in my youth no-one had a personal computer, let alone a supercomputer in their pocket as the kids do today. In my early days to 'play online' meant to go outside and swing on my mother's washing line while she wasn't looking. I was born in 1960, which was just after the first spaceship was successfully launched – Sputnik, by the Russians, but that was nothing more than an orbiting bleeper sending out a bleeping radio signal. No man had yet been into space, so nobody had seen a real picture of the earth before at any distance, incredibly.

I joined the mining industry in 1977 at age 17. One of the great things about that is when I first joined I got to talk to old mechanics aged nearly 65 that had been in the industry for 50 years. That took us back to times they could remember as far back at 1927. Of course now I too am in my late fifties, but if that ever bothers me I just think back to some of that old pit wisdom I learned from way back then. For example:

If you feel like an old fart remember that new farts aren't that much better.

The usual eloquence of the mines there, I am sure you noticed. Some of the conversations I remember with the old mechanics were about how to fix a car in the old days. When I say fix, I mean fix enough to sell it, so they told me all the dirty tricks. For example, if the car engine big ends were noisy then pour sawdust into the sump to make it quiet. Or later on, feeding a pair of nylon stockings into the sump which would bind around the big ends and keep them quiet for a while, long enough to sell it. There was no option for RAC vehicle checks in those days so anything criminal like this would not be easily caught. Of course nobody admitted to actually doing such dirty tricks themselves, but they knew of someone who did – the bad guys! However if it was your own car then you could of course do what you like to it to make it work. Looking back it is actually quite unbelievable to discover that car MOTs were not introduced until 1960. Before that if you could make the car work you could run it on the road, but I guess it was the state of some of the vehicles out there that led to the introduction of the MOT. In hindsight my old go-kart was a little too late for its time. Had I built it before 1960 I could have legally taken it on the road and blown off every car in sight in reverse. How awesome would that have been?

As an example of that kind of thing an old mechanic at the pit told me about a trick they used to deal with excess play in the steering. He had a car where the steering had as much as a quarter of a turn slack, which would be really dangerous as it would be difficult to make minor adjustments and it would wander all over the road. His genius way of dealing with that was to put 10 lbs more pressure in the driver side tyre to the kerbside tyre. That way the flatter kerbside tyre would always drag the car in one direction, towards the kerb, taking up the slack so you could steer it against the drag. He said that worked fine until you hit a pothole in the road, of which there were many, and then the car would be thrown all over the road until you wrestled it back under control again and the dragging tyre once again took over.

Of course these were the days long before seat belts. In my early days older cars didn't even have seat belts fitted. Also, one of the older cars we had had a bench seat at both the front and the back so you could legally pile in as many people as you could fit in the car. That could mean the driver would be crushed up against the driver side door while he was trying to steer and drive, and his gear lever would be on the steering column so the passengers you were crushing up to didn't get in the way of the gear change. For a while when my children were young I would take them to a kids activity group at the weekend. Other families found out about it and got their kids in on the ride so the car would be jammed full. As you can imagine the whole car was bedlam and the noise could be deafening. Then one day I was bringing them all home from their activity group and the whole car was silent, despite being jammed to the rafters with kids as usual. I got suspicious and looked in the mirror to see what was going on. I could see a myriad of kid's faces all grinning, and in the middle of that an unusual black face, all hairy with a big nose and teeth. The kids had smuggled a stray dog into the car with them. I had to stop and throw him out because he lived near the activity centre and not where we were going, but I could see him in the mirror running after the car with a stream of traffic behind him. In those days dogs also happily roamed the street alone, just like the children. Yes times have changed, and not necessarily for the better I can tell you.

CHAPTER 8

One thing I look back on in my life, about which I am eminently happy, is that my life was very physical. Of course this was the norm for any child, though these days things have changed somewhat. The virtual world is here and, let's face it, our kids spend a lot of time there now. For me that was not an option of course, though as my age shifted into double figures video games did first emerge in the gaming hut of the small country fair that resided on the edge of Sherwood Forest near Edwinstowe. The trouble was you had to feed the machine with money to have a go. I know for sure if I had free access to games like that in my day I would certainly have been an addict. I was only on two shillings (10 pence) pocket money per week at the time so video games were an extravagance for me, and I never felt good if I wasted my precious money or time on them. When I look back I am thankful for this because I now know what I would have missed in my active physical life that I enjoyed so much.

I have very vivid memories from my childhood that go back to before I could walk. Some of those memories really stick out. I remember crawling around the back garden of the house on Abbey Road in my red dungarees for the very first time, before I could walk, and having the time of my very young life in the long grass before the lawn was developed. Then I remember being sad the following day in my highchair because it rained and I couldn't repeat the adventure. I have other memories from my pushchair of black smoky steam trains crossing the railway bridge in the middle of Edwinstowe, serving the colliery, and of one occasion going to the train station nearby to see them close up. I remember my excitement at seeing Diesel trains emerge a little later on as that was the new thing at the time. That would peg me at just two years old. Sadly the big black steam trains with their smoke and noise soon disappeared after that, and I missed them, but hey, life moves on.

Aunty Edie must have clocked up some mileage on my pushchair in those days giving my mother some much need rest from three extremely energetic boys with a very inquisitive zest for life. Aunty Edie lived in the village. She was really my great aunt, the aunt of my mother. She was tall and slender, and the oldest and wrinkliest creature I had ever seen, with a stern look that was not helped at all by her then fashionable horn rimmed glasses. I hadn't heard of E.T. by that point, nobody had, but Aunty Edie was wrinklier than that I can tell you. My really abiding memory of her is one day visiting the pig sty near the Robin Hood pub crossroads and a pig was jumping up and bashing a board nailed over the sty window. Aunty Edie decided it was an emergency, that the pig may escape, and she 'spragged' herself against the board trying to hold it in place with the pig jolting her body every time it bashed the board. Even as a two year old I remember looking at this bizarre scene, trying to make sense of it, and thinking to myself 'that pig can't fit through that window'. Maybe my keen spatial awareness there was an early indicator of my gift for a life in engineering to come.

As I was saying, my life as a child was a gloriously physical one. I actually discovered full freedom from the day I learned to climb the garden wall to the road. There were few cars around on the council estate in those days so the danger was not like today. Much of our play was in the street. If a car did by chance appear, it was a sufficiently rare event for us to all stop and watch it go by with excitement before resuming our play. As I grew bigger we ventured further to the play parks on the estate. These were gathering places for a whole lot of action from all the kids on the estate. My mother, in an attempt to keep some kind of a handle on us and our fun, gave us a few guidelines. One rule was that we must always return home when the street lamp came on a few houses up the hill towards the play park – one that she knew we could see from the play park. That was a spark of genius from her as it saved her the need to come searching for us every evening as the sun went down. For us, however, it would always be a disappointment because when the lamp came on we were invariably in the middle of some creative adventure or other, and the lamp did seem to come on a little early before there were real signs of darkness. This is where again that spark of natural engineering talent seemed to kick in once again. On the way to the park we decided one day to shin up the lamp post and turn the bulb by about a quarter of a turn. That evening the light didn't come on so when we arrived home it was pitch dark outside. When we finally arrived mum looked really worried and began berating us for not coming home on time. We then came out with our ingenious defence – 'but the lamp post didn't come on'. When she ran outside to see the proof for herself she would return with a much more sympathetic attitude; we weren't such naughty boys after all, were we? After that the council would frequently be called out to fix the lamp, but strangely the new bulb never seemed to last very long. I once heard a neighbour talking to another whilst out walking the dog saying, 'Well, well, that lamp has gone out again.' I suppose for me this has to qualify as a long overdue confession.

After a few more years of good nutrition the estate was no longer able to contain us and we ventured out to the forests that surrounded us, and the river that ran through the middle of the village. In the long summer school holidays our energies never failed to find an outlet. Sometimes that meant damning the river downstream beyond the end of Boy Lane, near the base of the other railway bridge where the track left the colliery to join the main line. Here there were lots of stones and materials for the work. In summer we would literally work like beavers to complete it because that would give us deep pools in the river to swim in and a softer landing when we fixed a rope on a tree over the river and made a swing. I don't believe in reincarnation but if I ever do come back it may be as a beaver because that was a whole lot of fun, I can tell you. Every day we went there to the river intending to avoid falling in, but things never seem to go to plan do they? Early in the holidays, with a new swing in place, I would arrive home at the end of the day all wet and my mother would react with worried concern and outrage. Within a week or two though, I would arrive home and she would just glance up and say 'get those wet clothes off and come and get your supper'. I think she must have realised just what level of fun we were having because she herself was renowned as a tomboy in her day, spending many hours in and around the very same river.

Nowadays the world has changed. All the physical things we did were great preparation for the physical challenges of mining and life as it was back then. Today many kids spend a lot of time in the virtual world, but now I think about it, a whole lot of them will inevitably live their lives in that very same kind of environment. I appreciate the parallel. All my physical gaming made me fit for physical life. In a similar way virtual gaming often preparers them for life in our now computerized world. However, for myself, though I ventured into that virtual world in later years after mining, and even used it to make a living through making a connection from the virtual to the physical world by developing software, I still feel greatly blessed as I look back with the greatest joy and affection to those idyllic childhood years that were eminently physical in nature.

When I finally left school I did the usual and expected thing and went to find a job. I had pondered the armed forces – maybe the army. But by that time, though early, I was in a serious relationship with the girl, the daughter of a miner, who I would later marry. For that reason I decided to try to stay in the area. I looked at jobs in the nearby towns in the engineering factories, mostly where they manufactured some engineering product. In fact I was offered jobs in these places but it was on receiving these offers that I was forced to seriously consider what I wanted in life. As I mentioned before, there was an aversion in me to taking a job in mining. That came partly from the advice my grandad had given me never to go down the pit, but also from the fact my father had broken out of this lifestyle and become a fairly high flying engineer in the aerospace industry, as had my uncle Barry who was the son of the same grandad, the pit Overman. The first thing I did was compare the pros and cons of the jobs on offer. I knew I could always get a job in mining at that time if I wanted it. The factory jobs paid less, they required more travel, and the prospects for advancement were limited compared to mining. It seemed mining had the edge, but it was more than these simple practical details that persuaded me. There is something of an adventurer in us all, and this was certainly true for me. Mining is a huge operation. Though it descends into what may seem a very unnatural environment, there is something profoundly close to nature in it. I think at my core my soul craved nature, as it still does. Though it was more of an intuitive sense than a considered one, I think in the end my decision went towards mining because I felt it would better fulfil that deep desire for nature and adventure. As rough and tough as it is, mining is an epic adventure, and the scale of British coal mining was immense. Who is crazy enough to dig holes in the ground 1 kilometre down and up to 16 kilometres out? To handle millions of tonnes of coal and rock that has been where it is, undisturbed for millions of years? If Captain James T. Kirk thought he was the first to 'boldly go where no man had gone before' with his Star Ship Enterprise then he was very much mistaken. Joe Cole and his mining enterprise had been going there long before he even thought of it. Ok Captain Kirk may be right that outer space is the final frontier, but mining surely makes it to the semi-finals without a doubt. In the end my choice between this and a factory was no contest. Mining it would have to be.

CHAPTER 9

When I entered the mining industry I went in as an Apprentice Mechanical Craftsman in training. At the time there was a closed shop policy agreement with the mineworker's unions, meaning we all had no choice but to join a union. As for most, by default I joined the renowned NUM (National Union of Mineworkers), headed at the time by a man by the name of Joe Gormley. This was 1977 in the middle of a Labour government led by Harold Wilson, when unions were extremely powerful. Of course what everybody remembers most in the UK about mining is what came nearly 7 years later; the year-long mining strike from March 1984 to March 1985. By this time the government had changed to Conservative under Margaret Thatcher, and the NUM union leader was then Arthur Scargill who led the miners though the strike. This was at a time when the difference between Labour and Conservative governments was far wider apart in ideology than they are now. On the broader level communism was trying to stake its claim in the western world and in many cases unions in the UK were inclined towards those views. In many places unions in the large UK industries were led by people with fairly radical leanings in those directions. Of course back then, though after WW2 the west had given France back to the French, Italy to the Italians, and West Germany to the Germans, Russia had held onto its defeated nations in eastern Europe in the form of the Soviet Union, so the cold war was in full swing, Germany was split in two, the Berlin Wall was in place, and communism was well established in China and other countries of Asia. No-one knew where all that was leading – whether communism would eventually come to replace capitalism globally, or vice versa.

I was working in the mining industry throughout the strike years, mainly based at Bevercotes Colliery. At the same time I lived in Edwinstowe near Thoresby Colliery so in many ways I was in the thick of it throughout the strike. However my position was a little different to most because I was by this time training for management. A year after I joined the industry I was given the opportunity to aim for management. This meant shifting from the NUM to BACM, the mining management union. The deal between the NCB and BACM was completely different to the NUM. Management were charged with keeping the mines open and running, with no opportunity to strike. That meant if the men didn't turn up, all the essential jobs that must be done to keep the mine open must be done by us, the management. Those duties were both practical and legal. Inspections had to be made. Equipment that sustained the mine had to be monitored and maintained. Security had to be maintained etc. A mine cannot simply shut down completely, so to make sure the men would have a job when they returned to work we had to play our part.

Of course Nottinghamshire did not fully enter the strike, but they did conform to the overtime ban for that whole period so I was called upon to perform these duties every weekend during this industrial action. This demand to attend the mine during the strike did give me a unique view of all the action. In many ways that is true for most of my time in the industry because in some ways, though I had to go through a 9 year training programme that put me in contact with the workers all the time, nevertheless they all knew I was training for a management role and so could easily return as their boss one day – as some already had. Though my training was hands-on in every way, these differences did mean I sometimes felt more like a participant observer than a worker. Add to that the fact that the training was an intensive programme so I never stayed in one place for very long. This meant I got a broad view of the industry, but my feet never really had time to get rooted in any particular place or department until the last year or two after I finished the training.

For those who don't know the history of the miner's strike, most of the industry in the country chose to go on strike in obedience to the call of the NUM (union) under Arthur Scargill at a point when the Maggie Thatcher government decided to start closing some of the unprofitable mines. In fact she announced the closure of 31 unprofitable mines. In truth the whole industry was unprofitable with only very localised mines making any profit at all. This was simply the state of the industry given the global prices for coal. Why hadn't mines closed before now? One reason was the mind-set of the Labour government which was that the coal industry was a major employer and therefore worth subsidising to maintain employment, despite the fact that cheaper coal could be obtained from a number of countries abroad and there were other forms of energy available like gas and nuclear. Another reason was that Joe Gormley was a moderate with influence in the Labour government. That made the government more inclined to comply. Arthur Scargill on the other hand was a known radical and not trusted, especially by a Conservative government for whom he always made clear he held considerable contempt. Add to that there had been a great humiliation for the previous Conservative government under Ted Heath when the NUM forced the government to submit after the country experienced power cuts as the result of the earlier miner's strikes of 1972 and 1974. Anybody around at the time will remember that surreal period of candlelight every evening which was probably one of the greatest union victories of all time, and consequently a humiliating defeat for a Conservative government which ultimately brought it down and opened the way for Labour along with unions that now felt they were invincible.

Despite the call of the NUM for their members to strike in 1984, the whole of the Nottinghamshire coalfield was the main area that refused to comply and strike as they had in the early seventies. Officially it was not that they were simply defying the union, but they were demanding that the correct legal conditions be met before they joined the effort. That meant there had to be a National Ballot – a democratic vote for collectively deciding to strike – something the NUM were defiantly reluctant to do. Probably their main reason for their defiance on that issue was that the rules demanding there should be a national ballot had been introduced in the early 80's at the beginning of Maggie's premiership to curtail the power of the rampaging unions. She had also abolished the legality of a closed shop, all in the name of injecting more of a democratic process to the functioning of unions. No doubt the unions were indignant about this erosion of their power that previously to this had been quite totalitarian. The fact that the strike was called without a national ballot meant the government deemed it illegal, and that had the added effect of making the striking miners ineligible for benefits. Of course the well-known film Billy Elliot is about a boy from a mining village in Durham during this time who decided to become a ballet dancer, and the culture clash that caused. From my experience in the industry I can say that this depiction of the culture of mining communities is a fairly accurate one, though perhaps a little exaggerated. It also shows some of the deprivation the miners went through to sustain the strike for as long as they did. We are now about 35 years on from those events and the whole industry is now closed. Even at this range there are people with memories and strong emotions about that season. All I can do is offer the view of it I saw from my place in

Nottinghamshire, and my knowledge of it that came through either the grapevine within, or the media – the latter of which I acknowledge is not always that reliable.

Margaret Thatcher, as we all now know, was nothing if not determined. In terms of her politics she embodied the Conservative Party and in some significant measure came to define them for a while. In later years that led to some big blunders, but in the early years the country was in a mess, partly because of the dominance of unions, but also through excessive taxes and huge bank interest rates. When she first came to power she almost instantly pulled the rug on all the government financially supported industries in the UK, of which there were many. For a season there was a scary roller coaster ride every evening as the TV news programmes listed the many businesses that had gone to the wall each day. But in all of this, for several years she avoided any challenge to the mining industry, despite its deep unprofitability, other than the previously mentioned changes in the law on how the unions should operate. No doubt she remembered the defeat of the 1972/1974 strikes and realised the country was as dependent on the coal industry for power as ever. But she didn't simply ignore it. What she did was almost the opposite – she stimulated overproduction in the mines and the stockpiling of coal. Huge reserves of coal were built up, some of which I saw with my own eyes where mountains of coal were accumulated and then covered in topsoil and grassed over, as if to pretend it didn't exist. This was her preparation for the next showdown with the mining unions. She knew that all she had to do was close an installation and cause some job losses of union members to trigger another national strike, but she decided to announce 31 closures in the end just to make sure. The union leaders were completely intransigent on that point and ready to die to protect the job of every member.

Arthur Scargill was a Yorkshire man and former leader of the NUM in the Yorkshire region. As such he had the particular devotion of the Yorkshire miners. News sometimes filtered back to us in Nottinghamshire of the union problems management sometimes experienced there. Rumours abounded of Scargill in his Yorkshire leadership days, almost randomly ordering individual mines to strike at a given pit, just to show the mines management he had the power to do it. Of course they would have to find a legitimate reason to do so, but that is not too difficult given the many health and safety regulations we have to comply with, and the many agreements that have been made with the unions. All that is needed is a little creativity. In that way Scargill would flex his proverbial muscles to make sure the management knew who was in charge. News also filtered back to us of some of the union meetings taking place up there in Yorkshire. Some likened them to religious rallies where the talk at times had the distinct air of revolution. Very few Nottinghamshire miners were on board with all of that, and nor were the Nottinghamshire branch of the union. The radicals that the Nottinghamshire mines did have working there had often made themselves a little obnoxious trying to force their views on men that were more concerned with doing a good day's work for a good day's pay. Though all miners had their political views, and many naturally gravitated to the political parties they felt would represent them best, they didn't really harbour any national ambitions or a desire for revolution. In that sense they were much more moderate. Their views on Scargill and the union differed widely, but the general way of Nottinghamshire leant far more towards a person like Scargill's predecessor, who was a conciliatory man, than to one they felt wanted to dictate to them and the government with ideas of revolution on their mind. As I was in a position where I sometimes rubbed shoulders with management that had a role at national level, I occasionally got to hear the inside track on what was really happening. One of those contacts came in the form of a member of the NCB's union negotiating teams who knew Scargill personally and asked him directly what his ambitions were. He had already had a number of opportunities to become a British MP if he chose, but had declined, so the question was 'What did he really want?' The answer this person told me that Scargill gave him, was that his ambition was to head up the unions for all energy industries in the country. One thing is for certain, if this is true, had he achieved it then he would certainly have held revolutionary power in the UK. Of course some or all of this could be propaganda. There was much of that happening on both sides of the dispute. But in terms of the distrust the Nottinghamshire miners felt towards Scargill, it is a fairly accurate assessment of how they saw him.

Soon after the national strike was called and the Nottinghamshire miners refused to respond in the absence of a ballot, the striking Yorkshire men who now had time and spare energy on their hands headed straight for the pits that were still working to picket them. Those sounds and images I will never forget. Remember the film Zulu? When the sound of the hordes of Zulu's came filtering over the hills it was perhaps more frightening than facing them eye to eye. The sound of the picket lines at Thoresby Colliery could be heard in the village about half a mile away, and it sounded exactly like the African Zulu's. To cross those picket lines took guts, but many of the Nottinghamshire men were as defiant of the intimidation as the Yorkshire men were determined to intimidate them. Police were drafted in with the numbers needed to match the strikers. The one problem they had was they were not always sure where the miners were going to target in force next, so the police had to develop rapid response units. Special powers were given to turn the miners back on the roads before they even got there, given that the strike was illegal. Nevertheless many would always make it. I had one scary morning on security at Bevercotes Colliery when the lookout with binoculars on the main tower radioed an alarming report of a horde of pickets rampaging over the top of the pit tip towards the mine; again a scene reminiscent of Zulu. They descended on us in considerable numbers. Fortunately police were there within 10 minutes with dogs to round them up and confine them to the pit entrance. I have never seen anywhere transform from total peace to complete mayhem in such a short time.

Of course when the strike was in full swing nobody knew how long it would last – that was the scary thing, it was a totally unknown quantity. At about what turned out to be halfway through the strike there was some determined organised resistance began to gather in the Nottinghamshire coalfield to the ever more determined intimidation directed against them from union members and picketing miners. A story began to break in the newspapers of someone who gave himself the code name 'Silver Birch'. By this time the papers were almost universally against Scargill and the strike effort, perhaps realising that the ambitions of the man were revolutionary. It all began to seem rather dramatic, like some sort of spy novel, but I eventually learned the people in this group were people local to where I lived that I knew, some of them quite well. I was oblivious to this at the time but I had seen the one who turned out to be Silver Birch arguing defiantly in a TV debate that the miners should be given their legal right of a national ballot before the union expected them to strike. Unsurprisingly he was a blacksmith. One of the other members of this group was a really close friend. In hindsight I realised he was exactly the kind of person I would expect to be fighting for his rights. He was one of the contractor types I wrote about earlier who only took on the highly paid dangerous mining jobs. He wasn't the kind of man to allow anyone to intimidate him, and if they tried it was only likely to entrench him further, even in the face of personal danger. During this time he bought himself a 4.2 litre Jaguar so he could escape easily when chased by striking miners – something that he had been forced to do at times, especially after attending various resistance meetings. Sometime into all this, before I learned the identities of those involved, a car came racing down a road near where I lived, braked hard and a man in a pristine suit asked me for directions to the house of a person I knew. I asked his reasons and he said he was a reporter. Soon after that the story broke of the identity of this character 'Silver Birch' to be the man he was looking for, which no doubt led to some trouble for him. The Silver Birch code name came from his striking premature grey head of hair. I was aware that up until this point, and after these revelations came out, quite considerable finances were flowing into the hands of these resistance fighters, clearly from those who wanted to oppose the striking miners. The NUM never did call the ballot, and as a consequence the Nottinghamshire miners never did come out on an all-out strike, even though each pit did have its radicals that did comply, but they were very much a minority in Nottinghamshire. One inside insight I got from high level management in the industry on the national situation towards the end of the strike is that only the history books will finally reveal how close that strike came to bringing the whole country to its knees during that time. We have yet to hear the full inside story on that which I don't think will happen until the generations that participated in it have passed. After all, mining communities still exist, even if the mines don't, and some still harbour the raw emotions that the conflict evoked. As for my friend that was such a determined part of the resistance, he has already gone. Some years after the strike he was killed in a home accident, not related to mining, where an unbalanced grinding wheel exploded in his workshop and a piece of the wheel stone embedded itself in his brain. It didn't kill him outright, but that night he haemorrhaged and died. It was a tragic loss to his family and community because he was known to be a very strong and courageous man, though he always avoided the direct focus of the media so I don't think there was any egotism to his actions. When I reflect on it and remember him I have to think that the manner of his premature death does in many ways seem to fit the kind of life he lived – always on that dangerous edge. My point once again is that mining is an industry that creates characters like this, and to see that level of energy and determination clash as it did in the strike is quite a frightening thing. If that's the kind of grit we Brits are made of when put under pressure I think there is little wonder we endured and came through on the winning side of the world wars.

To keep things in balance, although the strike sounds like a whole lot of action, and it was, it was nevertheless punctuated with a whole lot of boring watching and waiting. There was the ever present possibility of invasion of the pit, but most of the time it was just quiet. Pickets at the pit gates would get bored, as would the police, so at times the spare energy of miners would naturally be redirected into some kind of banter or sport. One of the stories I heard of this kind of thing happened in the winter at a colliery nearby. The picketing miners decided to target a particularly chubby policeman. They built a fat snowman and put a toy policeman's hat on it. Then whenever this particular copper appeared from the security office there would be a whole lot of jeering and pointing at the snowman, with chants of 'Pig, Pig, Pig, Pig'. No doubt this officer of the law was instructed to ignore them, but eventually it got the better of him and he decided to react. He jumped into the police Range Rover and ran the snowman over. That would have been the end of that – another police victory, except that the pickets had built it over a concrete post.

Sometimes stories like this filtered through like they did for the trenches in WW2 where the men from both sides took time out from the war to play each other in a game of football. On quite a number of occasions the same happened between the miners and the police in their yearlong standoff. All in all there are more than a few similarities between the police and miners. They both do a tough, physical job, so naturally there was a certain level of respect developed between them. One key difference, however, was that the striking miners became increasingly impoverished over the year, and the police from all over the country made a personal fortune through all the overtime they worked that set many of them up for life. Believe me the government of the day were more than willing to pay whatever it would take to win this particular conflict.

During the strike year I got to know policemen from many forces around the country because they all wanted a piece of the action and the pay that went with it. As with the different collieries, I discovered the various police forces also have different cultures – some highly respectable and others that fancied themselves to be something like the TV characters in the Sweeney. In fact it was the London Metropolitan Police that proved to be the roughest bunch of them all. I guess that's just the nature of crime in the capital. One day I particularly remember was when we were quite bored as we had done our jobs and there had been no major picketing action for a while. Two Met' officers were there with us at the mine with their police dog. Then a call came through from these bored officers asking if one of us would be bait for the dog. They wanted some action as they were clearly missing chasing criminals across London, and the dog needed some exercise so they decided they needed one of us to volunteer to be the bad guy. I did think about it for about 30 mad seconds, but then discovered they had no protective gear but were planning to improvise it from some clothing they had found at the mine. It was then I decided to firmly decline with a few choice words. In the end they decided one of the coppers had to be the bait, even though the dog knew him a little, so they set about their exercise. Unfortunately the dog bit onto the coppers arm and his teeth slid down the padded sleeve and ripped his hand open. That was the end of the exercise and the injured officer had to head off to the hospital to get stitched up, but it did serve to break up the boredom a bit.

The strike was largely defeated through the vast coal stocks that had been stockpiled in preparation for the strike. Few in the country felt much sympathy for the miners cause in the end, even if they did respect the tenacity of the struggle. Since the strike there have been many closures. In truth many mines were way beyond their sell-by-date long before this. I learned this first hand when the coalfields started shrinking and the North and South Nottinghamshire coalfield areas were combined into one. That led me to visit some of those southern mines during my duties. They were mostly much older and shallower pits with much smaller shafts. The size of the shaft does have quite an impact on what machinery it is feasible to ship down there, and what coal you can get out. When I went underground I saw sights that I felt belonged in the history books, or came from behind the iron curtain. Relative to the more modern North Nottinghamshire pits they were comparatively running on chewing gum and string. The lack of investment was obvious. In purely economic terms these pits were probably decades beyond their usefulness, even if there were a few that could match some of the more modern mines in North Notts. In my view the actions of the miners were in the end perceived as so much of a threat to the country that the Conservative government that persisted for some time would have even closed profitable mines if they could and sought energy resources elsewhere. The lack of profitability for most therefore made it inevitable, but there was always the danger that miners would regroup and cause more trouble. Thatcher's way of handling this was clever, but ruthless.

When the strike was over Thatcher drafted in a guy to head up the NCB by the name of Ian McGregor. A Scottish-American industrialist who had a history of handling the kind of ruthless industrial overhaul that the government wanted. His strategic step was to identify the key operators in the industry – which was clearly the coalface worker. He then offered them incredible production based bonuses at a level they would previously never have been dreamed of. Suddenly the production of all mines shot up radically. You would think this would mean profitability, but the problem was the production levels were much higher now than the country needed. The government therefore made moves to shut the unprofitable collieries first. However, it was the vast money that men were now making that made them unwilling to strike again – it was a once in a lifetime opportunity for them. The face workers were now being paid handsomely, but the rest of the mine also got bonuses based on the overall production of the mine. Nobody could remember ever receiving wages at this level. It is rumoured that some of the face workers bought houses from the bonuses they made in these times. When money is paid out like that there is always a greed factor that kicks in, like the bankers of 2008, and that pay differential has the effect of dividing men and placing them at odds with each other. Those that are further down the food chain often resent those that are on the really high money and that has the secondary effect of causing divisions. Unions require men to stick together. When the wage scales were relatively flat money was not the issue. But once these pay differentials were created the unity of unions seems to crumble completely. Eventually of course the whole industry disappeared, but maybe the government can justify that by the fact that both the country and former mining communities have generally prospered with new jobs and industries emerging, and for many retirement was a feasible option due to the very generous redundancy payments. What local employers often realised was that former mineworkers were some of the best workers in the country having dealt with some of the most difficult conditions imaginable. A normal type of job was, and is, relatively speaking a comparative walk in the park, so that naturally led to whole new raft of industries arriving around these communities.

CHAPTER 10

As you will have gathered by now, much of my story is about mining methods and conditions, but a whole lot of it is about man management and the incredible challenge that it can be. In truth the number of workers needed and the types of big characters you meet in the mines means that this is perhaps the main part of the challenge, even beyond the technical issues. With that in mind I must give you an insight into some of the most interesting characters I met at the mines – the general pit Managers. This is the guy with overall control of a mine – quite a responsibility. That doesn't mean he is at the top of the food chain because there is an area level above him, and the national level above that. But in terms of the decisions on what actually goes on at a mine, the buck really does stop there.

I mentioned previously that each mine had its own culture. For that reason it was often better for a mine to have their own workers who were locally trained and for there to be little transfer of men between mines unless it was really necessary. That way a mine could develop its own workers to adopt and propagate that particular culture, and they would then fit in nicely. On the other hand, if you transferred men from one mine to another they would often take their culture and values with them. That could mean a mine transferring men with a work resistant ethos, to a mine with a hard working ethos, which ran the risk of threatening a successful mine with some real bad apples that would spoil the whole thing and threaten its profitability. However it was often the case that the really bad apples that emerged in a mine would get into trouble by their antics and be offered another job at a mine where there were already problems with the culture. This was the humane alternative to outright sacking because national industry rarely sacked anybody – if they lost this job where would they go other than on benefits, and that would just cost the government for no return?

Even among management you would meet a fair number of cases where the incompetent person is promoted out of the way to where they can do little harm. In this way, by transferring the bad apples to one place, they could be rounded up together, while the profitable mine continued to produce coal and sustain their pride and record of success. In some cases I saw newer mines that had begun on the wrong footing, in terms of their culture, because in their struggle to recruit men they had sometimes taken the bad apples from other coalfields and were finding it difficult to develop a good working culture in those places. These cultural differences would then demand a different form of management if they were to achieve any level of success. For places like Thoresby Colliery that had a marvellous time-honoured culture of respect, the type of manager needed there would be the eminent professional. Usually a gentleman that could be firm, but who knew the value of trust, respect, and delegation; a man who would respect the men, and who the men would in turn respect for his position and authority. However for mines that had a more anti-authoritarian culture, a totally different kind of manager would be needed, and it is these characters that really made my time in the industry quite colourful. Of course these managers also needed to command the respect of the men, but to achieve that they had to appeal to values that the men would accept. Given that the men were rebels, it could mean that the only person to whom the men would render any respect would himself have to be a rebel, like they were. So for this pit manager, rather than proving his respectability, he would sometimes seek to prove he was a bigger rebel than any of the men he commanded. This is where I have to introduce you to a pit manager at one mine who we will call Mr. W – he was just such a manager.

I heard one of the mining training personal I met on my travels suggest a vital qualification of a pit manager is that he must have the ability to swear continuously for twenty minutes without repetition or hesitation. Of course such a character would have to be very articulate, and in fact very intelligent, which is exactly what these managers were, including Mr. W. In fact to be really accomplished in the swearing department he would split words up into syllables and fit a swearword between each syllable. Of course swearing is endemic to every mine, but some clearly go the extra mile in this department and in fact Mr. W could drink and swear the rest under the table if the occasion demanded it.

With Mr. W, of course fighting or brawling was always another accepted value for men of the kind he managed. They would only respect someone who could back up their authority with the ability to slug it out the old fashioned way if the occasion demanded it. In truth a smart manager like Mr. W would not have to prove his credentials too often on this score because any event of this kind would be talked about by the men ad infinitum thereafter. So for a smart manager he would always pick his time, and pick his match. I therefore came to hear the legend of Mr. W down the pit getting into a blazing row with an official, and in the middle of the verbal onslaught throwing his stick down and shouting "right, let's sort this out here and now." That story seemed enough to convince the men Mr. W was willing to back up his authority with physical violence if necessary, which would be another box ticked, and also a great source of amusement.

Then would come his personal lifestyle. Generally the kind of thing we would be looking for here would be a James Bond type of character, or better. Mr. W was tall, blond haired, moustached, and devastatingly good looking – more boxes ticked. One day, during the strike, whilst on security at one particular pit, I had a call to say the manager's car was seen to be arriving along the pit lane – it was Mr. W. He would not expect to have to wait at the security barrier so my job was to make sure it was lifted before he got there so he could drive straight through. I lifted the barrier and as the car drove by it was the manager's car for sure, but there was a woman in it. I radioed back to say it was not the Manager in the car but a woman I didn't recognise, so my fellow security officer went to investigate. It turned out the driver was the Manager's daughter and the Manager was drunk in the back of the car – this was fairly early one weekend morning. At his request she had driven him to the mine, then rolled him out of the back seat at the mine. His intention was to ride on top of the cage to inspect the mineshaft with the Mechanical Engineer, who promptly refused to allow him to do it given his condition. Instead he went down the mine and walked for miles along the roadways to sober up. Again that week word of this incident spread around the mine and there was another box ticked on his curriculum vitae as a competent manager at this colliery.

Finally, we all know the reputation of James Bond when it comes to womanising. More than a few of the men at the mine had aspirations in that direction. Mr. W was known to be on his third marriage, but just to spice that up even more there was a story of him once taking his then current wife with him to the Miner's Welfare centre for a drink. That itself would be an extremely bolshie thing to do given that most managers would never be seen dead in such a place as it was quite definitely the domain of the workers. There in the Welfare his wife would suddenly throw a glass at him, which was unquestionably her response to seeing him looking up and down at the wife or girlfriend of someone else. He would then slap her in response, at which she would scream and storm off, and he would get on with bantering with the men who all found this behaviour highly amusing – even worth missing the latest episode of East Enders for. Of course, once again, all of this would be talked about at the pit the next day and ever after, and the end of it would be that every man would acknowledge Mr. W was the roughest, toughest and coolest guy at the pit, no question. The last I heard of him was he got promotion to area level and I saw him entering the area offices with pin stripe suit and briefcase, looking like he just stepped off a movie set.

I don't know what your reaction is to all of that: maybe shock; maybe amusement; or maybe both – I don't know. Whatever it is I can say that like a number of managers I met in my time, his style was unique and he was probably the best of the best at what he did. His style did actually seem quite effective. In hindsight one thing I am sure of now is that he was a very intelligent man, and more than a little of all this behaviour was in fact intentionally staged for the purpose of commanding what was a very difficult mine and body of men to manage. In any case it gave me a story to tell that definitely made my life quite colourful at the time.

To appreciate Mr. W's reasons for taking that approach I think back to another character that was training for mining management at the same mine. This was a young guy who didn't look physically equipped for a life in mining; he was not the sort to wield a hammer or any instrument like it, but he was academically gifted, which is also something that is needed in mining because the whole thing is a complex business in many ways and it needs the academic ability to succeed. However, when wielding a hammer shoulder action is always needed, especially at a mine given that in some mining villages if you have two whole ears they think you are a sissy. Elbow action with a hammer is embarrassing. And wrist action is decidedly camp having only comedy value at a pit, so that is not a distinguished start for a young manager. In the case of this guy it was interesting to see how the miners reacted to him. They liked him and endearingly nicknamed him *Petal*. In the morning, at the beginning of the day shift, it was quite funny to see him passing all the men on the way to their shift all saying to him 'Morning Petal', 'Morning Petal', with a big grin. The men accepted him and even loved him like they did anyone else in their own way, but how he would fare as a manager had yet to be proved. That said, I did meet a number of similar characters in mining management that persevered and eventually, through hard work and tough but fair man-management, toughened up and forced the men to render the respect to them that was due. So there are no fixed immutable rules about what makes a good manager. Each seemed to develop their own style and there are always some real surprises.

CHAPTER 11

One thing we all live with in life is a measure of danger. For myself, as a kid I seemed to attract it. It wasn't intentional, but was probably more a product of a certain amount of hyperactivity. Though my mother had 5 boys (before following that with 4 girls), she seems to think I gave her most of her grey hairs. I'm not sure if that's really fair, but I definitely at times got myself into the odd tangle. I suppose there is some evidence in the fact that in my early years in Edwinstowe I at some time broke every window in the rear of the house apart from the bathroom window. But even that was only because the bathroom window was too tough to break. My siblings broke none! Yep none! I used stones, balls, javelins and whatever else I could get my hands on, but none of it was intentional. In fact I would get myself into big trouble. My dad trained me on how to replace a window using the old putty method, and so whenever I broke one I had to replace it. Then I lost my pocket money for who knows how long to pay for it. But hyperactivity is not easily cured – sometimes you just do impulsive stuff and have to face the consequences.

It's worth remembering when you have children there is a 50/50 risk you are going to get frogs and snails etc. Sugar and spice and all of that is all very nice, but remember – this village needed miners. What I am trying to persuade you all of is – it was worth it!

The time we siphoned off petrol from Dad's motorbike to spread along the garden path to solve the ant problem was just part of the learning curve. How were we to know that fire would instantly spread from end to end of the path and the flames would be as tall as we were? Ok, we took the rap for it. We deserved it. But there was one time I nearly overstepped the mark in a big way. It came around my 9th birthday.

I was always inspired by the Sherwood legend and I begged and begged my parents for a real bow and arrow. Eventually, being the loving parents they were, they finally consented. In hindsight that may not have been the best decision given that this bow had 21 inch arrows with sharp points. My best bow so far didn't have much of a twang and the arrows only ever had suckers. What they perhaps didn't realise was that as a 9 year old I hadn't really grasped the subtle difference. This was the school summer holidays. My birthday was Thursday, but my Dad was at work. Knowing how much I wanted the bow my Mum gave it to me on time. My first act was to set up a target between the kitchen and lounge windows, with Mum at the sink washing the pots in the kitchen window and a brother watching the telly in the lounge. On reflection Mum did look a little apprehensive, like she was wondering if she had done the wrong thing. I also had a few misgivings but felt I had mitigated them by taking the suckers from my toy arrows and shoving them onto the new arrows over the pointy bit. The first shot went through one of the lounge windows, hit the curtain, and came to an abrupt stop when it hit the back of the telly. Unfortunately when the arrow hit the window it went straight through the sucker, so that was another misconception resolved. My bow was therefore confiscated until my Dad could give me some responsible guidance at the weekend. That was two days away; a very long wait for a hyperactive 9 year old, I can tell you. Anyway, Saturday did finally come and my Dad was more than a little annoyed at my escapades from two days earlier. I think he therefore decided to give me a lesson in patience and began taking ages arranging things – like sticking on arrow flairs, making sure they were straight, showing me how to hold the bow etc. He then decided he needed some glue for the arrow flares and had to go indoors to get it. So there I was with bow, arrows, and the unmistakable knock of opportunity. I realised another shot at a target would be way over the line, but the method I had always used to test my bows to see how good they were seemed to be the obvious solution. That was to shoot an arrow directly upwards and see how high it would go. I took my chance and made the shot, but then once again, for the second time this week, the unexpected happened – the arrow disappeared. It shot so high you simply lost sight of it. This was again a first for me. My previous bows didn't come close, and they had the added advantage of a sucker on the tip rather than a metal point. At that point instinct kicked in as I realised that thing was coming down – and that right soon. I therefore dived for whatever cover I could find. At that moment Dad walked out of the back door of the house. The arrow hit the ground a metre in front of him and bounced back up higher than the house. I am now 58 and have nearly recovered from the sore butt I acquired that day. As I said, danger is part of life. Most of it comes from the mistakes we make. The pit was the kind of place where those mistakes could really cost you, as that misadventure nearly did that day.

If I didn't say anything about the dangers of mining then I would not be giving you a real picture of what the mines were really like. There was danger every day. Health and safety in my day was strict. In fact it was stricter than at any other time in our history and more than any other country in the world. But that didn't prevent every accident. To try to combat the danger further there would be a whole lot of training for all the men, designed to raise their awareness of the danger. That was the best defence we had against accidents – awareness.

The most dangerous thing I knew of at the pit was on the coalface and it was something many miners worked with every day for many years. We called it the haulage chain. This was a chain that was slung along the 250 metre length of a longwall coalface and tensioned tightly so it hung in the air for the full length. It was anchored at both ends and the cutting machine would pull itself along the chain. Using the tension on the chain the 750 horsepower face cutting machine would haul its cutting drums into the coal ripping out a strip about three quarters of a metre deep for the height of the face, which may typically be about 2 metres high. The haulage chain had steel links each about the size of a man's fist. A steel chain like this is even heavy for a man to lift, but when these machines began to haul themselves along it would throw slack behind the machine as if it were pulling on a rubber band. That slack may then at any time be unexpectedly released and the chain would whip around on the face. To be as safe as possible men would always stay within the hydraulic chocks that had front prop legs so these would absorb the impact of such whipping and protect them. But there were the inevitable times, often when risks were taken that men took a blow from this leviathan. The chain could smash heads and sever fingers like a hot knife through butter, and on many occasions over the years it did exactly that. This situation persisted for decades with many losing their lives or receiving severe injuries through it, though in my time a track system was finally developed that eliminated the chain hazard completely. The machine then dragged itself along the track rather than pulling on a chain, which made the coalface profoundly safer, and it was probably the greatest safety improvement I saw at the mines in my time.

The chocks themselves were like a table with a top and a base, and 4 to 6 hydraulic legs pushing them apart. Each leg would have a force of 400 tonnes, so six legs amounted to 2400 tonnes of force keeping the coalface from collapsing. About 200 of these chocks would be set side by side along the coalface covering the full length of the face, a distance of about 250 metres. That amounted to a combined upward/downward thrust for the whole face of nearly half a million tonnes of force preventing the face collapsing. The coalface cutter machine, usually called a shearer, would sweep out strip after strip of coal and the whole army of chocks would slide forward, one by one, filling the void created where the coal was cut away, and leaving the roof behind the advancing chock unsupported so the roof could fall in in a controlled way. The roof behind would sometimes stand up unsupported for a while until the chocks advanced further. This collapsing area was known as the 'gob' and nobody in his right mind ever went there, except for the occasional foolhardy macho miner that did it for dare, I once heard.

Although a coalface could certainly be dangerous, if you kept to the rules it would normally be perfectly fine, and in some cases they could be a very fascinating places. I never lost the awe of seeing the immensely powerful coalface cutting machine ripping out strips of coal like tearing tissue paper. But beyond that there were other times it was fascinating. The geology alone held some real surprises. Sometimes the coal seam would undulate like a roller coaster. At other times the coal would disappear as the miners hit what we call a 'white wall'. This is a place where the rock has sheared along a fault line, so the coal seam disappears either up or down, and it was sometimes the guess for the miners as to which it was they had to go to follow it. At times we ran into fossil beds where there would be numerous fossils in the rock above or below the coal. If there were no breakdowns then as a technician you could often spend time splitting the rocks to discover the fossil treasures within; a fascinating distraction for a while.

Most of the time the rock underground is grey in colour. These are usually some form of mudstone laid down over the coal by water. However, on one rare occasion I was on a face at Ollerton Colliery where the rock above was red sandstone rather than the usual grey. This made the face similar, in a very broad sense, to an underground version of Miami Beach, which was a rare treat for sure. This red sandstone rock was very hard so the roadways at each end of the face had to be blasted with explosives. The whole process was slow so the face couldn't move forward very quickly, which in turn affected production. On this face the strength of the rock would sometimes mean the roof behind the chocks would refuse to collapse, and you could look a long way back into the gob where the coal had been removed. It seemed to just go on forever. Instead of collapsing the roof just seemed to hang there and bow under the immense strain. One thing that the law of gravity makes sure of though is that eventually this has to come down. The trouble was, when that happened it would mean hundreds of thousands of tonnes would come crashing down in a moment. Those miners that had been there to witness one of those mega collapses would sometimes be found to be absent from work when another collapses was imminent, such was the awesome and fearful power of it.

I said before, mining is a battle against nature. Even the routine of installation and maintenance is a battle. But sometimes troubles would come along that were really hazardous and they could threaten to shut a face, or a district, or even a whole pit if they got bad enough. One such hazard was gob fires. This could happen if the gob wasn't sealed well by the packs that the face men built at the sides of roadway behind the face as it advanced, so air would leak across the gob and come into contact with any coal that was left there. If oxygen came into contact with carbon – i.e. coal, a process of spontaneous combustion could occur which is effectively a fire, but not necessarily one that had progressed into flames. It was more like something smouldering, but it would be releasing harmful gases, like a fire, into the air stream and it would endanger the face, or the whole mine. Sometimes those fires have been known to produce flames and then there would be no choice but to take radical steps to stop it. All sorts of measures would be taken, and money spent to try to seal the roadway to stop the air leak, or dampen the fire in order to put it out, but if it failed it could threaten the closure of the face, again to stop the fire, and if that failed it could threaten the pit. Sometimes a face could be sealed just for a while and then reopened if the fire subsided, but if the face started up again there would always be the danger the fire would also start up again on the fresh air supply. The loss of a face would mean a huge cost to the mine and it would hit production badly.

The worst coal mining disaster in history occurred in a mine in Japanese occupied China in 1942 where a huge underground fire occurred and the Japs stopped the air flow and sealed off the whole mine with men still in there to try to put the fire out. That killed about 1500 Chinese workers and about 36 Japanese, most of them through asphyxiation rather than directly by the fire. Life was cheap there at that time and things mattered more to some of them than men, as we know from the wars that were in progress everywhere at that time.

One key to keep a coalface in good working order was to keep it moving forward, as fast as possible. Of course that was good for production too, so it was a good idea. For that reason breakdowns, dead shifts, weekend breaks, holidays and closures for fires and such could be a real threat because for some areas the weight of the millions of tonnes of rock above would come steadily down onto the face, like the hands of a clock moving, and the roadways would gradually crush and close up. This would particularly happen if you had already swept out another whole area of coal to one side of the face, as we often had. This same weight could come down on the face too, but the hydraulic support chocks were designed to yield as the pressure got to great. However, if that yielding ever got to the end of the chock leg's extension and it bottomed out the chocks would be permanently jammed into the rock and nothing would get it out other than a massive cutting operation through the face to free them. That would be such a big operation that usually in those cases the face and its equipment would be lost, at huge expense both in production and equipment. By keeping the face moving forward at a good pace these problems could often be avoided so sometimes that pace of movement made a high production pit even higher producing. All this meant any other kind of problem that halted the forward moving progress of the face could be a real threat.

One of those hazards that would bring a face to a halt was when the roof fell in and left a huge hole. It would of course depend where it happened and if the problem could simply be left behind. But if it happened in the roadway it could cut off a whole face, or many faces. I remember one such rock fall at a mine that happened on an important roadway junction. When the miners described it to me they said they could see the canteen ladies shining a light down to them from the pit canteen. I realised of course that this was just a typical comedic exaggeration on the part of the miners, but I decided to head down and see it for myself. The hole was immense. The only thing I could compare it to would be the underground halls you see in the mountains of the dwarves in the 'Lord of the Rings' films, but without the pillars supporting the roof. I thought the coalface that the junction served was doomed as I could see no way of fixing that, it was just too big. But miners are incredibly resourceful characters and the next time I went down there about a week later I could see a matrix of huge wood nogs stacked up like that game Jenga right up into the roof as far as I could see, which was as high as a multi-story building. I never got to know who did that job but it was astonishing to me that somebody had actually been all the way up there and risked their life to fix the problem. That was scarier than any shaft sinking job I had seen or heard of, but sometimes that is what it takes to keep the face open, the mine open, the coal flowing and the pay checks coming.

CHAPTER 12

The whole subject of geology is a fascinating one. Mining engineers study geology as part of their study curriculum, but most people that work in the mines are at least amateur geologist in some measure. When it comes to deciding where to actually dig roadways, we are talking about very expensive and important decisions that can cost, or even waste, millions of pounds. For that reason mines employ specialist geologists. Remember I mentioned the pecking order at UK mines – the miners rule as top dog, then come the technicians. Well there is a layer below this where the geologists live. They are clever and qualified people but they have the disadvantage of an impossible job. So much depends on their advice and decisions that they risk severe butt kicking with every roll of the dice. Yes, they can conduct surveys either by drilling or using seismic equipment. But this can be either very expensive, or inconclusive, which leaves them with a real dilemma. At times, to spare their aching butt, geologists were known to become highly political animals with a knack for survival. One pit Manager once shared with us a report that he had commissioned from a geologist which he had framed and hung on the wall of his office. It could be paraphrased to read something like this:

There might be a coal seam there, on the other hand there might not. If there is a coal seam there then it might be large seam, on the other hand it may only be a small seam.

Naturally the poor geologist became the object of ridicule thereafter so he may have been better off rolling the dice as normal and making his best guess. However, having given geologists a hard time I should remember the maxim that when you point a finger at another there are three pointing back at yourself. On that note let me mention the kind of blunders I came across in other technical departments, including my own.

Every mine had a Coal Preparation Plant, or washery, on the pit surface. This would be a multi-storey building, perhaps up to 7 stories high, jammed full of machinery for processing the rock and coal from the mine. They were exciting and challenging places for engineers. I would compare them to Willie Wonker's Chocolate Factory, except they were there to process coal rather than chocolate – sadly. I would also say another difference was that none of them had a Willie Wonker running them, but this would not be entirely true. Coal Prep Plant managers were an unusual breed that had their own eccentricities, so in a way they did all have their own Willie Wonker running it.

At one mine; this time Blidworth Colliery, the Coal Preparation Plant was a particularly complex spread of industrial plant that nobody but the plant manager understood, including the engineer who was responsible for it. The problem is, sometimes people realise they have the upper hand like this and begin to take advantage by defying authority and doing more or less what they want. One of the better jobs I had in my time in training, in terms of fun at least, was to build a scale model of this plant. This was before the days of computerized modelling (CAD) so the model had to be physically made, mainly from wood and Perspex. For that I spent a few creative weeks in the pit joiners shop. The idea was to give the engineer and others something they could use to better understand the plant and its processes without having to rely on the maverick plant manager all the time.

The purpose of the Coal Preparation Plant would be to wash the coal, separate out the rock and send that off to the tip, and sometimes to crush and grade the coal according to size of cobbles. I completed the scale model which had the main effect of confirming one fact; that this was one very complex piece of industrial plant. The reason for the complexity is that new processes constantly come along for coal processing, so the plants were gradually adapted to make use of these new processes. That may mean some alterations that would be entirely illogical if you were building the plant from scratch, but logical in terms of expense and practicalities when trying to append it to an existing plant. If possible it is always best to have a new plant, but this can be very expensive and time consuming, like building a new stadium for a football team. Blidworth Colliery was not such a profitable mine, with a very high rock content in their raw product (about 40% or more), so the plant was hard working and essential to the process. What I wanted to share was an engineering mistake that was made, as sometimes happens, but on this occasion it led to the engineer getting some really bad press about it.

A decision was made to alter the Coal Preparation Plant to accommodate a new process. As always this required building work, so the work got started. Then there was a change of mind on how the plant should be altered. The engineer ordered the current work to be stopped. However the building contractors then presented the engineer with the building contract that showed a penalty clause that covered the contractor for such an eventuality. What it showed was the cancellation meant the building contractors were set to make more money through the cancellation than if they completed the job. The engineer wanted this renegotiated but the contractors refused. In the end there was such a relationship breakdown that the engineer ordered them to continue the work and he booked the demolition engineers to demolish it. That meant at one end of the building the contractors were completing the building work, while at the other end the demolition engineers were demolishing the same work. This may have seemed the logical way forward for the engineer given the intransigence of the building contractors, but as you can imagine it led to the engineer becoming something of a laughing stock and gave him a whole lot of bad press which would probably have been better for him if he had avoided it by covering up the blunder, as normal.

CHAPTER 13

In truth mining in general is such a complex thing it is never normally a smooth process and a great deal of time is spent by engineers resolving problems that they inadvertently created. The NCB chairman, no less, once personally advised a group of us training managers not to stay in one place for too long because that way we could leave our mistakes behind us. Of course, to try to avoid as many problems as possible we were highly trained. My training lasted 9 years. As a nationalised industry the NCB were running the same government sanctioned training programme that was used in the Royal Navy, tailored for the industry in question. Part of the course ran alongside our studies at university for a B.Sc. (Hons) Degree, but it had to include the industrial element. The reality was the programme was so intensive it required a national institution of some kind to provide both the facilities and the funding for it, so it was only possible in an industry of this size. Within this programme there were some special management courses, lasting maybe two weeks at a time that were designed to test and develop our man-management skills. The idea was that if we are destined to make mistakes, which we all inevitably were, it would be better for us to make them in the training environment rather than out there in the field where it could be extremely costly. As a great deal of management focuses on the skills to communicate with people and lead them to cooperate to achieve a goal, many of these exercises were designed to test and develop those skills.

One exercise that I remember well divided the delegates into groups for a debating experience. The groups were all given the same real world scenario and told to debate their solution. They were then told to choose delegates to represent the group for the next round where each group was pitched against another and told to negotiate on their decisions in order to come to a common agreement on how to proceed. This would go on until the groups were reduced to just two, and the final debate would take place in front of all those of us that were not chosen, and in front of cameras with a view to analysing it afterwards. All these debates were conducted with a silent observer from the training facility whose observations would become part of the analysis.

The particular scenario we were given was of an aeroplane crash landing in the desert with us on board. The plane caught fire and we were able to escape, but were only able to rescue just a few items from a list we were given to help us come through the challenge of surviving the desert. We were told of a camp some 70 miles away, and that our radio was destroyed in the crash so we were unable to simply radio for help. This was in the days before mobile phones where such a situation would be serious and life threatening.

The group debates raged on, gradually coming to agreement on the items that should be rescued, until it came down to the final filmed debate in which I would not participate, but would be one of the many observers. What the delegates found on each side of this debate was that the items they selected to help them survive were completely different, so there was clearly some work to be done before they could agree. In front of most of the remaining delegates, this debate hit total deadlock. They simply could not agree on what items to keep and what to let go. Eventually the allocated time to reach an agreement ran out with no resolution.

Why did it break down?

Why were their ideas so different?

Nobody seemed to even ask this last and most basic question. The reason for the difference was because on one side the group had decided to escape the desert situation by walking across the desert. The other had decided to stay put near the crash site and wait for help. In short, their fundamentals were different. But this difference was never discussed. Yes, they both sought to survive, so they shared a goal. But they differed on the basic and most fundamental decision on what was the way forward in their quest for survival.

There was no definite answer to the problem we were given, except that afterwards the trainers suggested the recommended action would have been to stay put given that the chances of surviving the desert for a 70 mile walk, and then happening on the camp, were slim. Instead we would be better staying near the crash site and making ourselves as visible as possible to passing air traffic by laying out parachutes on the ground, and using flares and mirrors for signalling. These were maybe the best answers we could come up with but the problem was deliberately chosen to have no definite solution in order to provoke debate. How we would handle the conflict was the real issue in question. In truth, what experience suggests to me in hindsight is that this was perhaps the major issue for any mine managers because one thing was for sure, conflict was going to happen. In the end it is the ability to communicate and cooperate that decides the success of a mine, even beyond the technical challenges which were of course considerable. Then consider that within the mines there would be some really ambitious characters among their new mining managers. These were guys that were out to achieve something to prove themselves, so they would be competitive. Conflict would be unavoidable. What made it worse still was that after the strike the industry began shrinking so for a while the policy of the NCB (now British Coal) was to invent new management jobs by inventing new layers in between the existing tiers of management structure. After all, for mining engineers there are few other places to go than to a mine. Before long they were becoming like puddled ducks where the boundaries of responsibility began to blur and they were standing on each other's toes. For me, as part of the technical staff, there were some really challenging times when I got caught between these competing mining managers, who were the bosses, unable to please them all because they were at times each demanding opposite things of me.

In one such situation the mine in question had acquired a new, upcoming, arrogant, high flying mining manager from another area who was given the newly created title of Assistant Manager and he was determined to make his mark. His problem was he came up against an Undermanager that was running the show at the mine and had been doing so for at least ten years. As sometimes happens, these two began vying with each other for control of the mine. In truth the new Assistant Manager had the more senior role, but we all knew his was an invented position for which it was hard to define his responsibility. The Undermanager on the other hand was operating above the normal level for his role, but he had a network of about ten faithful Overmen whose allegiance had been secured over many years and he would meet with them all together every morning to gather information. What this Undermanager had learned was that information was power. If you wanted to put someone down, or to dominate them, then you could use information to upstage them before more senior management, thus undermining the trust senior managers would have in them. It was a political game for sure, and one that was hard to beat given the number of faithful recruits he had accumulated to his cause. Unfortunately I found myself unavoidably embroiled in this battle as each of them were giving me opposite orders, or if their orders were the same they each wanted to be acknowledged as the source of the order. Perhaps the reason I was drawing flack was that the Undermanager had got the idea I was favouring his rival, but in truth I was really trying my best to please them both. I guess even this was not acceptable in his view.

What this meant was that for 6 months I would get a phone call first thing in the morning, about 6am, where I would be interrogated, and if possible berated by this Undermanager while he had his ten faithful Overmen all present around him is his office with the speaker phone on to allow them to hear the conversation, each supplying him with information as he demanded it. You may ask why I didn't slam the phone down on this guy and get on with my job, after all at the time I had a department of 35 machines to manage weighing up to 87 tonnes, and the mechanics to go with it. In truth I did slam the phone down in frustration on one occasion, but that proved to be an ace card for him to take to senior management to show I was not cooperating, all confirmed by his ten witnesses. So I decided I had to tough it out, make sure I was on top of the job with the latest information, and stay calm in the face of every interrogation and comment designed to denigrate me or cast a shadow on my competence. This was very challenging and difficult early on, but what I found was I got better at playing him at his own game, though I had to be careful. The trump card would be to hold a piece of information they didn't have, which could potentially make him look a bit ridiculous in front of his ten accomplices; something that would usually raise his temperature to a point where he was incapable of a reasonable discussion and would therefore have to sign off and let me get on with my job. Of course there was always the possibility of me taking a more underhanded approach – of feeding him misinformation through his Overmen. But that would have been a dangerous thing to do and it was not a road I was prepared to even set foot on. All I was prepared to do was to hold cards in reserve for when I needed them. This proved to be a good decision; to avoid the misinformation, because a friend who was on the same training programme as me had done exactly this at another pit to which he was assigned. Bear in mind that we were both assigned to the pits we were at by area level, and any complaints would no doubt make their way back there. My friend was caught red-handed feeding opposite information to different mining officials at the mine having been egged on to do it by some of the wily staff that were training him who were themselves more experienced at doing it, and who knew how to avoid being caught. This meant he ended up on the Axminster before the pit Manager, after the officials shopped him, and he was then discharged from the pit back to the Area H.Q. in disgrace. When I heard about it I was glad I had decided not to go there, and realised it would be too much of a risk in any case as I was simply not clever enough to pull it off. One thing is for sure though, this was every bit as much a propaganda war on a mini scale as the East/West standoff was in the then cold war of international politics. Finally, after 6 months, the end of this trial came when one morning I answered every question/accusation that was levelled at me by this Undermanager who finally blew his top when I calmly said to him, after one extraordinary rant from him, 'I can't hear you when you shout that loud Mr. D'. At that point he slammed the phone down and never called me again. What always angered him was not that I didn't know the answers to his questions and accusations, but precisely the opposite; that I did have answers and he couldn't therefore pin me down in some way. I guess he realised how amusing it was becoming for his cohort when he got into such a state that he blew his top like this.

Regime battles like this happen often in the mines, and of course in most other industries too. This case was perhaps a little more extreme than usual, or it may just be that I found myself in the eye of that particular storm where he perceived me to be the biggest threat to his established regime. It seems to be a common thing that while people seek to be successful in their career, they also often hold another agenda of looking after their own interests first, even sometimes to the detriment of the industry they are serving. I met a lot of this in my time, but I am glad to say you also meet some that have their priorities straight and do everything they can for the good of the whole rather than themselves.

I left the industry before either of these characters – the Undermanager or the Assistant Manager, though I heard the Undermanager was in fact promoted to another mine I knew quite well as a reward for cooperating and assisting with the closure of the mine he had been helping to manage for ten years – that was how politics worked in the industry at that time. Though I don't know the details, no doubt he would not have had his devoted officials with him in his new appointment, so that would have meant he was forced to start at the bottom of the pile again. The last word I heard of him in that job suggested he had upset the men and become something of a comic figure to them who they simply disregarded. I am guessing he must have tried to operate the same way there, but I was familiar with his new mine and what I knew was that it had a different culture so the men there would only give respect where it was due. No doubt before long this manager retired on a decent pension and probably moved somewhere nice in his retirement. I certainly wouldn't begrudge him that despite my differences with him or my disagreement with his methods, but I can't say anything he did helped me perform in the job I was doing which was fairly critical to the mine. The last I heard of the young Assistant Manager was that as the mines in Nottinghamshire began to close he took an appointment with a company that developed mining equipment, but was fired after he upset them with his arrogance. No surprises there. I never heard anything of him after that but he was an intelligent and gifted individual who I have no doubt has found his way in the world, hopefully having matured out of some of that arrogance that was causing him so much trouble. For myself it certainly made me wiser and more battle hardened. It also helped me establish my department and gain some respect with my staff because, after all, many of my battles with this Undermanager were not just protecting myself, but also protecting my men from his antics and accusations. In the end I was glad to leave the place and begin a new career in software development, but this does give some appreciation of why the men that emerge from the mines always carry the mark of having lived and survived in that environment.

CHAPTER 14

In many ways some of the more colourful general pit Managers I have written about were people who had spent a lot of time dealing with men and had developed a sixth sense in how to manager them. I wrote earlier about Mr. W whose style was to be seen as the roughest, toughest dude at the mine, and so he commanded the respect of the rough, tough men that worked there. However, in his case he was more of a young high flyer, but there were other managers who had come up through the ranks, having done every job, and were recognised for their proven ability to handle the men. These were often guys that could be tough, but they were often also highly respectable individuals with a really tough edge to them. Take for example Mr. F who managed a mine I worked at for a while. He never shouted at anyone but had a unique way of reprimanding you when the occasion demanding it. Instead of becoming louder, he would go quieter and quieter, to the point where you were straining to hear him. That way he got your full attention because you felt you couldn't afford to miss a word he was saying or you would be back in the same spot before you knew it. These guys were the genuine rough diamonds.

On my travels within the industry on the national level I occasionally met managers who had developed an impressive reputation. One of these from another coalfield area was just this kind of rough diamond individual who had developed quite a reputation as a successful manager and I had the good fortune of the chance to ask him how he did it over a pint at a training facility where he was speaking in the hope he could pass his skills on to us. He told me how he initially rose through the ranks to get to be a pit Manager at some of the better pits in his area. Initially he was given the pit Manager's job at a pit that had never made a profit in its history, and was never expected to do so. But the year he got the job the mine made a profit, which immediately gave him something of a mythical status. How had he done it? Well, he simply decided not to sign any purchase requisitions. When his staff complained that they needed the equipment he simply said to them that the item they wanted was at the pit somewhere, so go find it. In this way he spent virtually a whole year with bare minimum costs while ever corner of the pit was salvaged for the necessary equipment and supplies. When it emerged the mine had made a profit that year he was immediately promoted to one of the better pits in the area, but he did give me a wry grin when he said 'I wouldn't want to be the guy that came after me'. Of course having stripped the mine bare, his feat was unrepeatable and the new guy would have to solve the real and more difficult problems there, which was to boost production.

I then went on to ask him how he went about boosting production because in those days this was more often a problem with getting men to work harder than it was finding some technical solution. This Manager then went on to describe to me one such occasion where the men on one of his coalfaces were slacking off and coal production figures were dropping. Of course the men had logical technical reasons for the decline, but on this occasion the manager was sure it was an issue with the men rather than the mine or conditions. The way he handled it was first to send his Deputy Manager down to the coalface to deliberately upset the men. When he got there the Deputy Manager basically criticised everything the men were doing, effectively calling them incompetent idiots. He then left with the men angry as hell and on the verge of a walkout, until they got word the pit Manager was on his way down just 30 minutes behind the Deputy Manager, so they decided to wait to express their grievance to him before they left on an impromptu strike. When the pit Manager arrived the men told him what the Deputy Manager had said to them, and of course the Manager was sympathetic and said (I quote), 'Did he say that? Well I wouldn't have said that to a dog'. He then asked them how they thought their problems should be solved and how they would make the face work, which they were more than happy to tell him in direct contradiction to what the Deputy Manager had said. The Manager then said to them 'Ok lads, I can see you know what you're doing. Go ahead and do it your way. Do your best.' The manager then left and that coalface hit record production levels in a very short time. This is what we would call motivational management. What the later bonus pay arrangements proved for sure is that when the technical problems are solved, this is what works, which is why production figures for all the coalfields multiplied in that time. I guess it's a little bit like the WW1 trenches where men sometimes get tempted to dig in and get comfortable. As I said before, mining is war, and it needs more than just engineering to make it successful; it needs motivation.

CHAPTER 15

One thing that never ceased to amaze me was the audacity of the UK national mining industry in that it seemed perfectly happy to undermine areas of land even though this was likely to cause considerable damage to surface property. This nonchalance seems to stem from several factors. First that it was a national industry and therefore owned by the government, which theoretically means it was owned by everyone in the country. Then the fact that the coal itself was considered to be the property of the crown, so it seemed reasonable that the government should be free to come and get it. Also in the early days of these mines there really weren't any easy energy alternatives so it seemed everything had to give way to the demands of coal production. Finally, much of the property we are speaking about was also either owned by the government in the form of council estates, or by the coal industry in the form of colliery villages that they had been built for the express purpose of housing miners. I think the industry felt the fact that they were state owned gave them the right to undermine any of these properties if they chose to do so. What changed everything, however, was the decision of Maggie Thatcher's government in the early 1980's to sell off all council houses and colliery houses to their long time tenants. Then suddenly the whole issue of undermining and causing subsidence became a hot political topic because people who owned these properties expected to be compensated for the subsidence damage. The trouble was in many cases the damage was already done, but it often takes a number of years before the effects of undermining to show on the surface. In many cases the mining continued because there was no certainty that it would cause subsidence, or that if it did there would be the necessary drive and will to take the industry to court to obtain the compensation. However, like the recent PPI selling scandal, the chickens did eventually come home to roost in the form of lawyers ready to take a 'no-win, no-fee' gamble on it. The reason for that is that the government have always been a sure bet when it comes to payment. Not only are they guaranteed not to go bankrupt and therefore to come up with the cash, but the levels of compensation that could be claimed through them would also be higher. Subsidence therefore became a very expensive issue that demanded huge levels of back pay for the undermining that had already happened over the years. Of course it is not possible with mining on this scale to avoid all property damage. Some of it had to be seen as collateral damage to be absorbed and accepted, but there was always a whole lot of wrangling going on between property owners and the coal industry as they tried to minimise the costs as far as possible.

One effect of the subsidence problem in the early days of this was that the coal industry would keep their plans close to their chest and would only expose them to interested parties when forced to do so by law. All that said, it wouldn't be fair to say that the industry didn't care at all about subsidence. During my training I went to one colliery where I was shown a map of the plans of what coal reserves were due to be mined. The map showed outlines of the surface buildings in the area, of which there were only a few in this case. I then noticed that one of the coalfaces was due to end in a particular place, but I could see no reason why, so I asked why there were no plans to continue and drive the face out further. The staff member that was showing me the plans then pointed to a small outline of a building was about 400 metres further on from the place the face was scheduled to end. He then said 'See that?' I said 'Yes'. He said 'Do you know what that is?' I said 'No, what is it?' He then said 'That's the house of the coal board chairman for the area' who he also named. Of course he didn't say any more and left me to draw whatever conclusions I could, but that conclusion was that the industry definitely did care about undermining property in some particular cases.

In the North Nottinghamshire area two of the mines out of the 15 were responsible for more subsidence damage than the whole of the rest of the coalfield put together. These were Mansfield Colliery, and Sherwood Colliery, both of which are in the area of Mansfield, and Mansfield Colliery was responsible for twice as much subsidence cost as Sherwood. In some ways this was unfortunate for them because when these mines were first sunk they were much further away from property, but the urban sprawl of the towns over the decades had meant buildings had reached the colliery and passed it by the time I came to work the coal reserves there. When subsidence became a big issue that led to all sorts of attempts to mine in ways that caused less damage, such as mining short 40 metre length 'Shortwall' faces instead of the usual 250m 'Longwalls'; leaving coal pillars that it was hoped would help support the surface and prevent subsidence. Also mining very low seams of higher quality coal that it was hoped would help maintain profitability was another solution they tried. In some cases it helped, but not enough keep the mine profitable. In fact these mines were always loss makers but when you factor in the subsidence costs the losses became considerable and unsustainable, which in the end meant they were the first in the North Nottinghamshire area to close.

The lowest seam I ever worked on or visited was at Mansfield Colliery in Nottinghamshire; it was 28 inches (0.66 m) high. Men would work full shifts on this coalface. At times I went to do some job on the face, or prepare and plan for some maintenance, so I had to crawl along it. It was 250m long, but given the room taken above and below by the hydraulic chocks, as a 6 foot tall guy there was not enough room for me to crawl, so I had to belly it. Then once when I reached about 200m, close to the far end, I discovered the roof had partially caved in so I had to turn around in that space and belly it back to the roadway where I had entered the face. For some even a 2m high coalface would be a challenging experience, but this was on another level of scary to anyone with any claustrophobic tendencies. Consider then that in the Welsh and Scottish mines, until very recently up to that time they had been mining seams as low as 15 inches (0.38 m). To get this coal out they would be forced to mine a few inches above or below the seam but those conditions are really unimaginable, yet men worked in those conditions for full shifts at a time for all their lives. At times miners would banter about the conditions like those Monty Python types of sketch humour – 'when I were a lad' – where they would exaggerate everything. Their forms of comedy were to claim they worked on a 3 foot high coalface in 4 feet of water; or that the seam was so low if they took their shovel in upside down they couldn't turn it over to use it. They also worked long shifts. Remember the old line in the Monty Python sketch that they worked shifts so long that they had to get up half an hour before they went to bed. Personally I think the reality was so tough it really didn't need any exaggeration whatsoever. In my mind those miners that worked in those conditions were heroic, nothing less, which is why their relatives really need to appreciate exactly what was done for them in those times. As I've been saying over and over, mining is like all-out war against nature.

CHAPTER 16

There's one thing for sure, by most people's standards life underground is a tough one. Moles seem to like it of course, and good luck to them, but they have a few evolutionary adaptions we don't. One thing war does for soldiers is to make them appreciate the value of peace. For miner's they get the same kind of contrast when they return to the surface on a warm sunny day and get to enjoy nature again. The contrast is wide. You often see miners in their spare time, or after retirement, out in the countryside enjoying nature to the max. Many are fishermen, or own dogs and love to walk. Sherwood Forest is one of those places that appears to be the perfect antithesis to a mine. Mines are full of dead rocks, mostly grey or black, and even though the coal was once living it has been dead for millions of years so a mine is the really tough side of nature. Add to that the industrial grind of it all and it can seem quite oppressive to some. The contrast between that and the natural living colourful trees of the forest is huge, so the beauty of it is much more keenly felt after a hard week of grafting in the mine.

For myself I always had a connection to nature having grown up around so much beauty. I spent virtually all of my spare time in it as a boy – playing in and around the rivers, walking, climbing the trees. For a while one fashionable sport was squirrel catching. A pet shop once offered me a price for every squirrel I could catch for them. I never took them up on it but I did acquire pets for a few friends. Squirrel catching is a bit of an art. Not something I would do now as we have all become more ecologically friendly, but in my early day those things were not really on the public agenda like they are now. Eventually I learned the do's and don'ts of how to catch a squirrel and I have the scars to prove it. My knuckles look a bit like I was once a street fighter with the scars, and it was sometimes useful in a pit environment to let people think so, but the truth is the scars on my fingers are mostly from squirrel bites.

Squirrels are not really vicious animals. Usually they only bite if you scare them. Otherwise you can grab a squirrel and it will just freeze. The times I got bitten were before I realised this and I would climb a tree and either get the squirrel cornered hiding in a hole, or chase him to the end of a branch and then start whipping the branch around until he fell off. If you got him in the hole you could get a hold on him but if it still had somewhere it could look to run, and it could hold on with its claws, then you would be ok, it wouldn't bite. The big mistake was to pull it out of the hole or peel if off the branch so it had nothing to cling to – then it would curl up and bit every time. I gradually developed a method of ripping the squirrel off the branch and quickly transferring him onto my leg where he would cling on until I was ready. Then quickly ripped him off again and, before he could bite me, dropping him into a coat below that a friend would be holding open ready to catch him. You just had to do it quickly enough before he had time to bite.

During my school years I once took my first girlfriend on a squirrel hunt without divulging what we were actually doing. I thought this would be a good surprise for her. When I got her holding the coat open at the base of the tree and she saw me grab the squirrel she finally realised what was going on and went on strike. I really didn't understand girls in those days having been raised as one of five brothers. My sisters were only young by then so I was still on that particular learning curve. I was still at school at the time so I guess that is forgivable. In time this girlfriend came to love nature as much as I do, which was something because she had been locked in her back garden all her life. I find girls with older brothers get a fair amount of freedom; or did do in my younger days. That's because they have brothers to look after them. But if the girls are the oldest or don't have brothers then sometimes their mothers are highly protective of them so they don't get much fun exploring beyond the garden wall until they're older. I of course was free from the time I learned to climb the garden wall aged two. This was just how it was for this girlfriend when I met her, though I didn't fully realise it. Naturally I felt the best thing I could offer her was an introduction to the idyllic life I was living out there in nature. What finally converted her was a particularly good day of fun which came on one of our very first dates.

We went to walk the banks of the local river. When I say river, it is called the River Maun, but it is really more of a stream. Some people think to qualify as a river it has to be something like the River Trent, but that's all semantics really. My definition of a river was a watercourse that you couldn't jump over with your best long jump – something I tried and failed at a few times with this river. If you could jump it then it was a stream. The River Maun was a bit too wide to jump over it, though there is a place a little upstream of Edwinstowe where it passes through red bunter sandstone that it can be jumped fairly easily. Nevertheless in my eyes it was still a river and I spent much of my young life in it with a Tom Sawyer or Huck Finn type of existence. The river flowed past the bottom of our garden in Ollerton and I learned on Sunday mornings they always opened the dam upstream at the mill to let the flotsam go and then closed it again which stopped the flow for a while. At that point the river would stop flowing and the fish would get caught in pools. I would then spend a couple of hours trying to catch slimy slippery eels with my hands. A time or two I got caught in the river when the water began to flow again and the river rose quickly over my wellies before I could escape. Anyway, as I was saying, I took my new girlfriend on a walk down the river and on this occasion made a very rare and fortuitous find – a car roof. This river wasn't one of those that is filled with shopping trolleys like you find in towns or cities, but on this occasion I found a car roof that was sunk on the bottom of the river. When I re-floated it I realised it was made to be used as a raft. I then found a bucket that had also floated down to use for a seat and me and my initially petrified girlfriend boarded it and floated down the river. We went for about four miles, over weirs and rounding corners, and at one point came across a brood of ducklings that decided to dive and swim underwater to get away. Unfortunately for them the current was flowing at the same speed they were swimming upstream so I was able to pick the ducklings out and plonk them on my girlfriend's lap. Wildlife experiences like this were quite usual for me, though this adventure did turn out even by my standards to be a pretty good day. What I didn't realise at the time though was that having been locked up all her life in a garden, for my girlfriend this was an out-of-this-world experience. From that point on she was addicted to the countryside as much as I was, which did seem like a great start. At least nobody could say I didn't know how to show a girl a good time.

In my time involved in squirrel catching I became a fairly experienced tree climber; something my mother assures me I aspired to from a very young age. This just gave me a whole lot of experience. Then in my early teens I saw the film *Kes* about a boy who found and kept a wild Kestrel. From there I began to keep Owls and Kestrels that I acquired from nests I found tree climbing in the wild. It's not something that would be acceptable nowadays, as I was saying, because we are all much more ecologically aware now. Back then it was not really seen as a big issue.

I kept different birds of prey for about five years as a teenager. They would always return to the wild within a year, but not before I had a whole lot of fun training them for a while. The first bird I had was a Barn Owl I named Barney, and he was a true character all the family came to love. He particularly loved the piano because he could stand on it and feel the vibrations through his feet. If he flew to the piano and nobody got up to play it he would decide to play it himself and jump down onto the keyboard and run up and down the keys. Occasionally he would give visitors to the house a real fright by taking off and landing on their shoulder. I sometimes used to ride my bike with the owl on my back, wings spread into the wind clearly enjoying every second. I had to laugh at one guy I passed that looked really alarmed and shouted to warn me I had an owl on my back. I always gave these birds lots of freedom and the house I lived in was situated in a perfect area for them. When I had a Kestrel I would release it at lunch time and then when I got back after school I would go out of the back door to feed it. The back door looked across a field so I would invariably see a Kestrel flying towards me eager for his dinner. Then one day I went out of the door and couldn't see the Kestrel, until I felt a draft of wind and looked up to see it hovering just above me waiting for me to raise my glove. Eventually, inevitably these Owls and Kestrels would grow up and one day I would be unable to get them back to their cage because they had eaten enough, so they would find a nice branch in a tree and spend the night outdoors. I came to understand that a few days after this happened they would suddenly be gone – partly because they realised there was food out there to be caught that could feed them, and also I think because their mating instincts would kick in so they would go off to find a mate. One special treat I had one day was to climb a tree I was familiar with in the forest where I knew there was often an owl's nest. When you come across a nest with newly hatched chicks the maternal instinct of the mothers would sometimes be so strong they would stay on the nest, even though really frightened by the invasion. On this occasion there was a beautiful female Tawny Owl on the nest with every colour of brown you can imagine in her plumage. She spun her head around and looked straight at me but seemed quite calm, so I put my hand into the nest to lift her up gently by her wing; enough to see the chicks beneath her. Her response was to twitter a bit and pull her wing back, but strangely there was no evidence of fear as there would normally be with a wild bird like that. I believe this owl was in fact one that I had raised, which made it a very special treat for me that day. Of course I left her to raise her brood, but did see them again later when they were close to flying.

CHAPTER 17

As for many miners, nature was the way I recharged my batteries after the sometimes gruelling environment down the mines. Eventually you get used to the hardship of it, but I did get an insight into what it was like for those who weren't conditioned to it.

After I left mining I joined a software development company working on virtual automotive engine and gearbox design and analysis software. I worked for a company with Chinese owners and they had clients over in Asia. One time we had a visit from two South Korean engineers from Hyundai. The boss of my company asked me if I could give these engineers some kind of local industrial experience. I therefore contacted a pit Manager I knew and arranged a visit to Thoresby Colliery. I gave them the full experience, taking them to the coalface. They gave us the full treatment. At the face the miners decided to demonstrate to them the mechanical action of one of the hydraulic chocks advancing. This means lowering it off by realising the upward pressure of 240 tonnes, then pulling it forwards to advance it to where the coal had been cut away, and then resetting it in the new position. This face was about 2 metres high and had the very latest technology which means the control systems had advanced so all this happened at the press of a button for each chock. The men invited one of the Koreans to press the button. Of course he didn't expect what was about to happen but when 240 tonnes of pressure is released and a piece of equipment as heavy as this moves, the noise and vibration is so loud and scary it sometimes seems like the whole earth is caving in. This engineer took fright and ran down the face for his life. Then when he realised nobody else was running, but just laughing at him, he came back looking rather sheepish and wondering if he was really worthy of his black belt in Karate. In hindsight I should have prepared him better, which I did try to do, but there is a politeness to Koreans that makes them reluctant to keep asking when they don't understand. I guess on this occasion he wished he had better understood my attempt to prepare him for was about to happen. When we finally arrived back at pit bottom the other one of these engineers hung his head In his hands and said in his broken English 'That was the worst experience of my life'. I had quite enjoyed the trip down memory lane, but I do appreciate what it must be like to encounter mining like this for the first time, especially when your only experience has been that of an office and a car factory. Believe me, he saw the very best of mining there. The worst, I am sure, would have totally horrified him.

CHAPTER 18

One thing I have to cover about the mines is the danger. Without it the picture of life as a miner that I am giving you would not be complete. At this point I have to advise anyone that is a little squeamish to move on and skip this part because I have to be a bit graphic about the things I saw and heard to give you a real insight into that aspect of mining. In truth the modern mines were as safe as they could be, but that was built on a horrific history of accidents, often fatal, that led to all the modern health and safety legislation. When young miners joined the industry the knowledge of how to survive is drilled in to them like an army exercise until it is certain they know everything they need to know, which is quite a challenge because some of the lads that joined were in no way academically inclined so getting any amount of information into their heads could be difficult. On that issue I found the training centres, like the one at Lound Hall near Bevercotes, were real training experts. All credit to these trainers, they took their role very seriously and did an incredible job of preparing the lads for the mine.

Historically what made mines extremely dangerous was the industrialisation. Fragile human bodies never stood much chance against solid steel; a lesson that has been learned many times the hard way. At least in war you know people are throwing steel at you to kill you so you can take precautions, but in mines it invariably catches you off guard and hits you unexpectedly. I think back to stories of when pumps were first introduced to drain the mines of water. This was near the beginning of the industrial revolution. These pumps were installed near the mine shaft on the pit top and they would have a long beam overhanging the mine shaft and a steel or metal pump shaft would run the full depth of the mine shaft. The pump shaft would continually drive up and down as they drove the pumps in the pit bottom, with a stroke length of about 50 feet. At the same time men would be accessing the mine by climbing ladders up and down the mine shaft next to it. Then someone had the idea that if you attach platforms to the pump shaft, and aligned other platforms on the walls of the mine shaft at the ends of each stroke, then you could let the pump shaft lift you out of the mine in stages by stepping onto these platforms, letting it lift you by the stroke length, and then stepping off onto the static platform and waiting for the next pump shaft platform to come down on the next stroke, alternately transferring from mine shaft platform to pump shaft platform, and vice versa as you rise. Bear in mind that the prospect of climbing a deep mine shaft on a ladder at the end of a full day of work as a miner was a gruelling one so anything that eased the pain of that was welcome. However, to ride up a mineshaft clinging to pump shaft like that, and stepping on and off platforms at exactly the right moment was a very precarious thing to do. As a result many fell down the shaft and were killed, or were injured by the moving machinery that would stop for no man. Miners, being the characters they were, would still take the risk but the death toll was considerable. There were also times when the pump shaft broke under the load leading to the inevitable considerable loss of life for those riding it.

Later, as mines got deeper winding equipment was added which was safer, but to say it was safe in the early days would be an exaggeration. Even later on Markham Colliery near Bolsover in Derbyshire was infamous for an accident where the cage plummeted down the shaft to the bottom with men inside. All were killed and that was enough to strike terror into all miners because all rely on the winding equipment. As normal, in response the safety regulations were tightened to the point where they became the strictest in the world, but that was never able to stop all the accidents in mineshafts completely. They are very simply extremely dangerous places to be. Sometimes you hear genuine horror stories from mines abroad where the safety regulations are not as tight. One of those is of mine where the winding of the cage was in complete control of the winder rather than controlled through automation. If he made a mistake and overran he could plunge a cage full of miner into the pit bottom sump which was full of water and all the miners would drown. At times he would just overrun a bit and dip them up to their waist or something, then lift them back up. If this happened, when these men got back to the surface the winder would be running for his life across the pit yard with the men chasing him intent on killing him or at least giving him a good bruising. Trust me, this is not fiction.

One very effective method that safety training officers always used to train us how to survive in a mine was to scare the living daylights out of us with stories of accidents. One story was of a blacksmith at Mansfield Crown Farm Colliery before I worked there. When machinery or long girders don't fit in the cage to go down the mine the way to get them down the mine was to sling them below the cage, so the cage would travel high into the headstocks so they could be dangled beneath and then lowered down the mineshaft. On one occasion at this mine the girder was hanging over the shaft ready to be lifted and the signal was given to lift the cage higher to pick it up. Somehow there was a mistake or miscommunication and the cage went down instead of up, hitting the overhanging girder. At this moment there was a blacksmith standing straddling the girder on the side of the shaft. The girder reared up and flung the blacksmith high up and into the shaft where he fell half a mile to his death. That was scary enough but the really gruesome message was that a leg and parts of his body were found jammed into the gutters on the way down as they had been ripped off as he impacted them as he fell. When a body or an object falls down the shaft it doesn't fall straight. As soon as it hits anything from there on it will bounce from wall to wall all the way down. The chances are this blacksmith would have been knocked unconscious long before hitting the bottom.

Another story I found really chilling from the safety officer was of a coalface worker at Sutton Colliery some years earlier that was operating an old face machine called an undercutter. This had a jib arm for cutting a gap at the base of the coalface so the coal could drop when it was blasted – this was at a time early on in mechanisation when the coalface was routinely blasted to get the coal out. This jib would swing side to side. The miner who suffered this accident was known to the men as Bill. He made a mistake and attached the haulage rope that pulled it along to the wrong place on the machine causing it to flip so the jib arm with its cutting teeth flung back towards him like a giant metal crocodile coming down on him several times as it flailed about. In these cases you often wish the man was killed outright, but not in this case. The safety officer that told me about this was very graphic about it – he wanted the story to have the maximum impact so I would heed the warning. Bill was carried out of the mine. He had a pencil jammed into an open artery where his arm had been severed off and his rib cage was split open. At this point Bill was still alive and the men could hear him repeating to himself 'I am not going to die, I am not going to die.' The medic that attended him took one look then took out a large needle and threat and stitched his clothes together just to contain his organs. Bill died 15 hours later. This kind of story was enough to make anyone like me very vigilant when working in that environment.

These of course were the second hand stories passed on to scare me for my protection, but as I said you can never eliminate every danger so every miner sees a measure of this kind of thing themselves. I worked with some blacksmiths and fitters in the mine shaft at Welbeck Colliery on several weekends, installing a pipe range down the shaft. That meant I got to know the men quite well. Then one week when I was not scheduled to go there was a similar miscommunication as in the Mansfield Colliery case. The cage sped off up the shaft by mistake dragging a pipe with it. One of the men was standing in front of the pipe in an inlet to the shaft that was 60 metres above pit bottom. It dragged the pipe and knocked him down the shaft. In this case he hit the wooden boards at pit bottom and miraculously lived, but not without the loss of a leg which took most of the impact of his landing. I saw him back on a pit surface job a year later, but it was clear he was severely traumatised. My guess is he demanded to return to work, otherwise there is no way he would have been there. He was a former Karate instructor so this case seemed particularly tragic. The cost of mining work can be incredibly high, even ultimate.

On another occasion I was close to the end of a shift and a call came in that there was a man trapped in the mine but there was nobody nearby to help because it was the end of the shift. We quickly grabbed all the heavy lifting equipment we could carry and sped down there. There was a green light all the way – pit cage waiting, loco waiting at pit bottom to rush us out there several miles, then we had to run with heavy equipment and chains for about half a mile. When we got there it was a 19 year old lad that was trapped under a 6 tonne machine that had fallen off a pallet they were loading the machine onto. Fortunately the machine had crushed the lad into the side of the roadway where there was a slight indentation in the rock strata that had saved him. Nevertheless the cutting picks had smashed ribs and the leg bones of one leg were both snapped like a twig. We lifted the machine off him, I administered pethidine and we got him out alive. He was very fortunate not to be killed. With him was an older many who had panicked and frozen when the machine toppled and he heard the screams, he also with a minor injury. It traumatised him so much he was unable to even look to see how this lad was – he was clearly expecting him to die. One year later I saw this young lad again working on the pit top in the pit baths. He had a bad limp which he would have for the rest of his life, and a lifetime of financial compensation, though it was a high price to pay for it. The main thing is he survived. This accident happened because they loaded the machine on a side that had a gear wheel sticking out. When they tightened the chains they were using to secure the machine to the pallet it turned the cutting head, which rotated the gear wheel, which made it ride on the pallet and surge sideways, falling off the pallet. A memo had been circulated some time before on this very danger, but getting it to the people who need to know can be a real challenge and omissions were sometimes made. Sometimes it is the lack of a tiny piece of knowledge like that can cause nasty accidents. In any case, even without such knowledge, miners had to have a sense that helped them survive and take precautions in these circumstances, but there is always potential for accidents like this.

Of course there are numerous stories like this, but that is enough for my purpose here; to give you a real appreciation of the danger of the mines. But even with this danger there is sometimes a funny side to it. I once saw a miner on the coalface get a cut on his head. His mates came to sympathise with him – yeah right! When his mate saw the cut his jaw dropped and he said OMG, like it was really serious. The injured guy then turned white with shock, at which there was an outburst of very raucous laughter. Don't get me wrong, if it had been serious these guys would have moved heaven and earth to save their workmate, but anything less worthy was seen as yet another opportunity for sport that would become the main laughing point at snap time or that evening at the Miner's Welfare. They say all is fair in love and war. Personally I would include mining in that. No doubt this kind of behaviour is not limited to miners. In fact when I was making the Coal Prep Plant scale model I spent time in a pit surface joiners shop at Blidworth Colliery. There they had a stuffed monkey as a mascot. Whenever anyone chopped the end of a finger off, or bumped their head, the monkey would soon appear sucking his finger, or with a big bandage on his head. As I said, anything less than near mortal injury seemed to be fair game for a bit of sporting banter.

CHAPTER 19

Talking of sport, it has always been a very keen interest and topic of discussion for miners, as it seems to be for all working people with physical jobs. I think the physicality of the sport is what they relate to, and the concept of a staged battle that in some weird way reflects the battle of life we are in, including all it takes to win a living in this world. Most of the kids I grew up with came from mining families so that competitive survivalist gene seems to have been passed on to them. For me it was a little different. My parents were interested enough to watch England in international football games, and they had an interest in tennis as this was a sport they had both played, but there wasn't the same priority to sport that I saw in the parents of my friends. In fact as we didn't get a television until I was eight years old, I was raised without even seeing much sport in my early years. The keen interests of miners seemed to be football, rugby, horse racing, pigeon racing, darts and snooker, but of these football was by far the leading interest. After all, the local top flight team was Nottingham Forest and they happen to have achieved what could be considered the greatest achievement in the whole history of British football. That was winning the European cup for two years running in 1979 and 1980. What makes that so spectacular, given that others have done it? Simply that this is a 'provincial' team rather than one of the usual big hitters and the European cup was the equivalent of the Champions League back then – the highest accolade in Europe for club football. It was the inimitable Brian Clough that led them to the victory, though with the backing of the brilliant football mind of his friend and colleague Peter Taylor.

Brian was the manager and very much the front man for the team. He was famous for his big head and loud mouth, whereas Peter was much more behind the scenes and a little shy of the cameras. Just to give you a typical quote, Brian was asked on TV by Parky on his chat show if he thought he was the best manager in the country. His reply was:

'I wouldn't say I'm the best, but I'm definitely in the top one.'

Another time Parky asked him how he handled disagreements with his players. Brian said:

'Well we sit down together and talk about it. Then when we've discussed our differences we decide together that I was right.'

Then there was the time the fans invaded the pitch after an important win. He was so angry he grabbed two of them and punched them in the chops right in front of the cameras. The media latched onto it and gave him a hard time trying to turn it into a big deal as usual, so he invited the cameras in to film him meeting the two supporters he assaulted to apologise. When it came to it what he did was give them a parental ticking off and then said to them 'Come and give Uncle Brian a kiss' so they both had to give him a kiss on the cheek. That was how Brian dealt with the media. Perhaps it was the sheer 'bolsh' of the man that made him appeal to the workers. It was something they could relate to. Anyway, a statue now stands in prime position in Nottingham centre as a testament to his popularity. If you want to get more of a feel for the character then watch the film *Damned United*. It is refreshing to see he could also be humble when the occasion demanded it.

As I was saying, for me and my brothers we were not raised playing football as some of my friends were. That made me a slow starter, which I think was also true for me academically. At school I was the kind that would drift off into my own thoughts a lot and so miss the lesson. I caught up later, as with the football, but it took a while. My argument about the academics was that nobody ever told me why I went to school and I didn't figure it out myself until I reached age 14. How was I to know you were supposed to work at school if nobody ever told me? That's my excuse anyway.

With the football I reached the end of Junior school aged ten and still had very few football skills. My year had a football team; a good one, but naturally I was not part of it as I was known to lack the skills. Then in our final year of Juniors my class was challenged by the school year below us to a big game, just to see who was best. The stakes were high, but with kids that age a year of growth makes a lot of difference so it was a bit of a giant killing attempt on their part, all made more challenging by the fact ours was a top team. I went to watch my mates play after school, but then they realised they were a team member short so I was invited/coerced to play. Feeling wanted for a change I agreed, though a little apprehensively. I didn't even have the boots for it, just my school shoes. But the team assured me I could stay in defence and I wouldn't see much action, and so it turned out. I spent the whole time without seeing the ball, except at a distance at the other end of the field. Then, after many hours, our team reached its target of winning 50-nil. Yes 50! At this point they decided that the victory was decisive and maybe it was time to go home. Then someone asked out of the blue 'Have we all scored at least one goal?' Even the goalie had scored because they had swapped goalies during the match so everyone had scored – except me. At this point they decided to keep playing to complete the victory and turn it into total annihilation, complete with bragging rights, so I had to score. They then stood me in front of the opponent's goal and said 'You stay there and we'll pass the ball to you, then shoot'. It sounded simple enough, so for a while I got chance after chance to bury the ball in the net, but each time hoofed it in the wrong direction. Then someone was fouled in the penalty area – it was a penalty. Of course this was my chance. I took a long run up and again hoofed the ball at the net to the best of my ability. This time it was on target, but the goalie saved it. Then came my moment. I ran in and hit it on the rebound straight into the back of the net. My whole team erupted with cheers and I was buried under the pile of celebrating players. It was probably that moment that gave me a passion for the game. That was the only goal anyone seemed to talk about the following day at school.

My excuse was that my feet were too big for me when I was small and it took time for me to grow into them. They are size 12 now but much more in keeping with my stature these days. Joking aside, in the end I did come to learn to play football well, and remarkably I did it from a reading a book. A beloved aunt, Ruby, on my Dad's side used to buy me and my brothers a Rupert Bear annual every Christmas, but when we grew a bit bigger she decided to branch out and bought me a George Best comic strip book with instructions on how to practice and play football. I took it seriously and spent hours doing what it said. In the end I got to be as good as rest, once even scoring a 40 yard goal in a match which was the only time I ever saw a whole football field stop and clap.

I actually still use football to keep myself fit to this day, aged 58, but this is the story of my humble beginnings with the sport. Who knows what you can accomplish if you put your mind to it. Academically the story was similar. I caught up bit and achieved a few results, but then stayed at school for a year to get more qualifications. Then I joined British Coal as a Craft Apprentice, but my academic ability was spotted and I was given the chance of a student apprenticeship, eventually achieving a B.Sc. (Hons) degree in Mechanical Engineering at Trent Polytechnic (now Nottingham Trent University). I have to be thankful to British Coal for that opportunity – I was very fortunate. That achievement then defined my life because I took on the knowledge and skills I learned to become a software developer, started my own company, and developed engineering software for the sheet metal industry that is now used around the world.

Many of my peers in the industry also went on to do similar things when the coal industry began to close, all based on the excellent training we received through British Coal. A training that I doubt we could have received anywhere else in the UK, or indeed the world.

Getting back to the sport, my point was that miners love it. It provides a real outlet for their competitive aggression, both in the form of playing in Colliery teams, and watching the sport either live or on TV. The subject could fuel conversations for the whole week in the mines so to be a miner you really needed that interest to fit in. Of course collieries are also famous for their Brass Bands, and their singing – especially in Wales, which does show there is a really creative side to hard working miners that needs an outlet as a welcome relief from the daily grind of work. But daily grind it is, and anything that prepares you for it helps. Football was one thing. But by far the thing that prepared me most was Rugby.

My Rugby days started in my school years at Dukeries Comprehensive School, New Ollerton – now Dukeries College. It drew in all the kids with some level of physicality and the will to prove it – many of them from mining families and with Dads enthusiastically driving them on. I was built for strength so I found my natural place among the forwards in the pack – the scrum. Believe me the forwards in a Rugby team are the guys at the coalface. They have to be everywhere yesterday, so they have to be strong but all able to run continuously and fast, so the action for them hardly stops. There is a pile up everywhere the ball stops moving and they are ones that do the piling. The game develops a real team mentality and teaches you controlled aggression. One unexplainable truth of Rugby that each of us had to discover for ourselves was that if you go in soft you get hurt, but if you grasp the nettle and go in hard you usually come out unscathed. What it means is 80 minutes of pain – often at your limit of endurance.

I was positioned either on the second row to give the big push, or if I wanted to see more of the action on the field I was loose head prop (on the left). The loose head prop is not bound into the pack as tightly as the tight head prop on the right so he gets to escape quickly and be part of the action. That position was tough on the shoulders as you lock horns in the scrum with the other team, but it gave me many scoring opportunities to run in a try so the reward was worth it. If anything was going to prepare me for the environment of the pit, it was this. We had a great team. I recall some massive winning scores of 93-3 and 78-0. There was only one team in the county we were outclassed by and they were all blacks – meaning they were all black kids with the strength and physique that nobody else in the county could beat. It's good to have a nemesis like that. It makes you work hard to beat it, even though we never did.

After any game of Rugby, usually on a Saturday morning, I would limp home and soak in a hot bath. There was a feeling to it that has to be 'felt to be telt' as the saying goes. When you got there you just knew your work was done for the day and all you could do was rest up and recover from all the knocks and bruises you picked up in the match – most of which would be back in order or well on the way to repair by the time you came to the next match, if you were lucky. I think the Kiwi's famous war dance at the beginning of a New Zealand match depicts the inner attitude you have to get into to win at the game. And the same goes in many ways for the daily grind of working on the coalface at a coal mine.

CHAPTER 20

One thing I saw a lot of in the mines was the tension between bosses and workers. Of course men vary widely in their motivations and commitment. Some take their job really seriously and devote every hour to it, though in some cases excessive overtime was a sign of trouble at home and the pit was their escape and safe haven. For others there was a different reason. I remember asking one young guy why he worked so much overtime and he said he had two wives, two dogs, and six kids to support. That was a divorce case. He was trying to pay his dues to his former wife and family and at the same time maintain a high standard of living for the new one; a very common story even for back then which meant he was working every hour God sent.

Of course all of the personal details of fellow miners were a huge and never ending topic of discussion, even more so than the sport. For example there was the guy who was kicked out of the Salvation Army with the full ritual of sword broken over the knee, for running off with the Lollipop lady. That kind of story was more entertaining for the guys than any of the soaps you see on TV. The rule of thumb was always to try to keep your personal life to yourself because if you accidentally let something out it would spread through the pit like wildfire, and you were then fair game for a laugh.

Sometimes it got more serious though and you felt with some their lifestyle at home meant they were living on the edge of breakdown all the time. For some it was part of their image and street credibility to be engaged in some of these kinds of shenanigans. Often you would hear of wives that were living it up in that way too, so whenever their man was tucked away down the pit she would feel free to pursue her extra interests. Of course the great news stories for the lads would be the times when someone was caught at it. The problem was that before Thatcher forced the sale of the mining houses the mining housing estates were exclusively miners, so these kind of activities were happening in a microcosm environment. That made it difficult to get away with anything without being spotted. It fact these estates had a whole culture of their own. Many didn't even venture out to the local pubs but spent their drinking hours in the Miner's Welfare that would also be exclusively for miners, often situated on these same estates.

When Thatcher finally forced the sale of these properties to their tenants they got a fantastic deal, though many were really outdated with outdoor toilets and coal houses built into the house. However the sale of houses meant they were the cheapest and most affordable on the market so from 1980 or so onwards many young people from outside the industry came into the estates and that did begin to break down that exclusively mining culture which in truth has to be said to have become a little dysfunctional, inbred and separatist. Soon the influx of everyone from yuppies to old folks made for quite a cultural change that I think was mostly positive as it integrated mining communities back into the rest of society.

At times I heard and saw some of the tragic cases of domestic breakdown. One shift manager got a call from a worker in a far reaching location in the mine to say he was about to hang himself. His wife was notorious for her activities while he was at work, keeping a china bull on her bedroom window sill. If the bull was facing rear end out then she was open for business. As soon as the call came through men were despatched to try to reach him and prevent the tragedy, but when he saw the lights coming in the distance he decided to go ahead and do it, so by the time they reached him he was dead. This is just a snippet of the kind of thing you see and hear about, and I guess it happens everywhere, though I think with miners there was sometimes an inclination to live dangerously on all fronts.

One other episode of my life I prefer to forget about involved me finding myself the first on the scene of a murder in a domestic situation where the guy, a miner, had tried to live the kind of life that is often promoted involving an 'open' relationship lifestyle. Then when his partner got seriously involved with another guy he realised he couldn't cope with it and it led him to commit murder in a frenzied stabbing attack. It is a fact that 98% of murders happen between sexual partners. Only when I went to court to testify did I realise more fully the tragedy of it all. The young man that lost his life was just 23 and dearly loved by his family and community. As a neighbour I knew the guy who committed the crime to be a nice guy, but he got in over his head with his misconceptions of life. He had a previous altercation with his rival where I had intervened but he had broken his nose. I tried to warn him of the path he was now on but he assured me it was all over now he had done that. Only days later came the crime. He had unleashed forced that seemed beyond his control. It is something I will never forget and it made me wake with a start for a long time after whenever I heard any bumping in the house.

After that event the house of the neighbour passed to relatives as it was difficult to sell it with the stigma attached to it and for a while it became the haunt of drug addicts and the like until I caught one of them burgling houses on the estate and called the police to come and arrest him. This was not the normal kind of trouble we had back then. Before the police arrived I had a bit of a life chat with him about his direction in life. Later I met the same guy again who thanked me for nabbing him and said it changed his life for the better – he was then happily married so his life had changed quite radically. The police also gave me a commendation for the act, which was nice.

Just ten years later I was shocked to bump into the guy who committed the murder, now out on a license. I was just walking along the streets of a city and there he was. I didn't think I would see him again for a long time, if ever. His behavioural record in prison was so exemplary he got out in record time, confirming what I knew about him. The problem with him was more to do with domestic misconceptions that were passed on through his mining culture and of course the result was tragic for everyone. These stories are all a harsh reminder of how tough life can be on the domestic front.

There is no question life has its troubles. True for some more than others, but none of us escape it. After all life is a terminal condition and we all have to face that. It can be bereavement, sickness, financial troubles, relationship troubles and a host of other things. I had a very difficult season when I had a swimming accident on holiday and nearly drowned, despite the fact I am a very strong swimmer. I just pushed it too far and ended up having to be fished out of a pool with my lungs full of water. That led to a chest infection that the doctor misdiagnosed as a simple cough, which before long led to hospitalisation right at the beginning of my final year of degree education. The result was a partial collapse of the infected area of one lung; a condition I could still feel nip deep down inside for four years if I breathed deeply. I was back to work and study as soon as I could make it, within a few weeks, but it left me lethargic and weary, and that led to a very difficult academic year. Then when I went back to the pit I had the stresses of the combative undermanager I wrote about earlier which together with my lung condition recovery gave me considerable stress that led to ulcers for a while, though I concealed all that from the men. In the end I really needed to leave the industry for a physical rest because that final year had been a gruelling one. That led to a better season but there were more pressures to face with running a business through times of recession that soon followed. After mining I was present in hospital when my father died after three strokes over ten years that first took his speech, then his mobility, and the final one led to his death. Also for five years after mining I took a part time job driving the emergency doctor around Mansfield and the surrounding area, including my home villages. Then later I ran the emergency doctor's department at Newark Hospital for a while. That meant I saw a lot of suffering, as doctors do, including a number of occasions where I was present with a family as their loved one passed away from some terminal condition.

Well, no-one said life would be easy. I feel like I experienced the full gamut of life's challenges in my time. It certainly had the effect of forming character along the way so I am not complaining, just being honest, and though I have made lots of mistakes I have no regrets. I always remind myself there are people around and in the world that have it much worse than I ever did. For some that would be a reason to abandon any faith in God or anything like that. But for me I had faith, I am a Christian believer, and later I will share something of the background to that in my childhood and how it affected my mining years. In all of the trials and struggles, and the ugly things that happened as well as the good, I see a purpose in it all so my outlook is quite upbeat and optimistic. I guess I always had the sense that this world is a temporary residence and none of us are here to stay, so to look beyond it has always been a natural thing for me, as I think it is for many of us when we look up from all the many distractions.

CHAPTER 21

As I was saying earlier, there is an ongoing tension between workers and those that manage them. In the general case in such a physical environment workers want to perform but don't want to be overstretched. To work at 110% all the time is a sure recipe for breakdown – it's unsustainable. For that reason there is always a certain amount of cat and mouse chasing going on by the department managers who feel the pressure to get the work done, and the workers that are trying to manage their energy resources. That means there is always a certain amount of either push-back which never looks good, or smoke-and-mirrors to throw the bosses off the trail. If there was a way to string a job out many would take it. Of course in such a game there are always some that take it to an extreme. They become clever at dodging work rather than doing the job. I am currently thinking of two chock fitters that were on permanent night shift, who the men came to call Rigour and Mortis. They just had a talent for dodging work. One night I saw one of them appear to be working quite hard re-arranging some flexible pressure hoses. I was impressed. Or at least I was until I realised he was making a hammock out of them.

On one occasion while still a craft apprentice I was deployed with a mechanic to inspect the bearings of the main fan that ventilated the mine. The fans to a mine are huge because they have to draw air through miles and miles of roadway. The diameter of the fan is probably about 4 meters or more. On this particular job the mechanic had me acquire a huge bag of rags, from which I deduced this was going to be a very dirty, greasy place. We had to take off an outer plate to the fan housing by undoing a whole array of bolts, removing a hatch plate, then crawl through the hole. Then we had to weave our bodies through the fan blades, and then take off another hatch plate to the central aerofoil and climb through that to access the centre where the bearings were. He then took off the bearing plates and did the examination, after which he replaced it – job done. I then wondered where all the dirt and grease was. He then explained the bag of rags was his pillow, and mine was the tool bag. We then had a good hour or so of extra sleep. Or at least he did. Mine was a bit too lumpy. I guess he figured no boss would voluntarily climb through the assault course we had gone through to get to where we were and so took his chance to catch up on some much needed zzz's after the early start.

Occasionally in the mines you meet characters that are a complete one-off, the likes of which you are never likely to meet again. One such character I came to know went by the name of Fred. He looked as old as time, bald on top with white hair. He was stooped and had massive hands and feet. His hands reminded me of the buckets on a JCB digger. He had a number of blue scars on his head. These are scars from a cut where coal dust got into the wound and it was not cleaned out fully, so it healed over with the coal dust still in it. He seemed quite clumsy so I guess that made him prone to accidents like that. The miners nicknamed him Jed Clampett after the character from the TV show the Hill Billies. That was because he used string to hold his trousers up like Jed did, apparently.

The other thing about Fred was he was really tough. I guess a life of clumsiness does that to you. When he walked he kind of lifted one foot at a time like he was lifting a lead boot, and threw it forward firmly planting it before taking the next step with the other foot. Those feet and huge boots must have been really heavy. He lived in my village as a teenager and my mother befriended him.

For Fred any attention was always very welcome as he clearly didn't get much. No positive attention anyway, as you would expect working at a pit. That said he was a very happy soul and he used to sing to himself all the time, even though he was completely tone deaf. He was once reputed to have walked into the local veg shop, singing as he went, and grabbed an old lady and danced her around the veg stall. She turned out to be Lady Manvers – a local aristocrat from the nearby stately home, Thoresby Hall. Rumour has it she loved it so much she went back the following week for a repeat performance, but that is probably just pit talk.

The whole village knew Fred, mainly because he rode a bicycle. That in itself wasn't so unusual but it was the way he rode it that made him stand out. He would wander all over the road, especially when carrying a 56 lb bag of spuds on the handle bars, as he often did. One day he came to visit my mother and began to tell us stories of all the atrocious drivers in the village and all the accidents they had caused him. I can't remember ever having to try so hard not to laugh. In fact, to be quite honest I laughed, but it didn't seem to bother him. After the bicycle he then got himself a moped. In truth I think that was a little better. At least I never saw him carrying spuds on the handle bars.

One incident I feel really bad about was one day when I was fixing a car over our garage pit I needed to test the car after some repairs to the engine so I went for a 5 minute drive. When I got back I parked the car back over the pit again and went into the house, and there was Fred looking a little bit worse for wear. It turned out he had arrived at the house on his moped and decided to park it in the open garage. You guessed it. He didn't see the open pit and fell into it, motorbike and all. He then crawled out and made his way to the front door of the house where he rang the bell. When my mother opened the door he just said 'I need a stiff drink sister'. I swear he was indestructible. I felt really sorry for my part in that by leaving the garage open and pit uncovered. I really should have known better. But we retrieved his moped and fixed it, and Fred was ok, so I guess it had a happy ending.

Sometime later after I joined the mines a pit Deputy told me a story of a guy that was deployed to the coalface where he was in charge. This turned out to be Fred. The Deputy knew he was down there so when he did his rounds inspecting he was surprised that he didn't see him because it is hard to miss anyone when you go along narrow roadways and a tight coalface. Later, back on pit top, he asked Fred where he had been and he said he went to the face as deployed. The next day the Deputy decided to make sure he found him. He went through the whole face and roadways twice without seeing him. Then, on his third pass, he walked past an ordinary length of conveyor and just saw a tiny glimmer of light beneath the conveyor. There was Fred laid flat beneath the bottom belt of the conveyor, catching up with some sleep with the moving conveyor only inches above his face. While the belt was standing he had dug himself a hole to crawl into where he could spend the shift. As I said, he was a one-off character. Fortunately for him nobody ever got sacked from the mines when it was a nationalised industry. They just got a good ticking off and for a while deployed somewhere undesirable in the mine as punishment, which I guess is a bit like the Russians sending their dissidents to the Siberian gulags.

I did feel bad about the car garage pit incident with Fred and his moped, but I can assure you that is not the only stupid blunder I have made in my life. Take for instance the time when I was at college and my motorbike kick start lever sheared its splines so it just hung limp and wouldn't work. The only way to start it was a push start, and that was hard work. Not having the money for the repairs as it was a case of engine out, I decided to weld the kick start permanently to its shaft. Then it would work and I could fix it properly at my leisure. As a mechanic you have to make similar temporary improvisations a lot at a pit given that you are often miles out underground and need to get the job going before parts or equipment can arrive, so even this was good for training. If you couldn't do it then it could cost the mine hundreds of thousands of pounds in lost production revenue.

As I was welding away with the bike flat on the ground I heard some screams. I removed my welding mask to see the bike on fire. Unfortunately you can't see normal flames through an arc welding mask, only the welding arc. The screaming was from my mother who had seen the flames and had a bucket of water. I had to shout 'quick throw it on' so she did, which put the fire out. I had made the mistake of leaving something flammable beneath the bike – rooky error. The fire burnt out the battery charging electrics so the only way it would work after that was on the battery power after a home recharge. The problem was when the battery was getting low it had some funny effects. When you turned the indicator on it robbed the ignition power and the bike would involuntarily slow down as the indicator blinked on, and then surge forward as it blinked off. I gave a friend from college a ride as a pillion passenger one time when the battery got low. It was very hard to keep the bike stable with the indicator making the bike slow and surge like that, and him rolling about laughing about it on the back seat behind me.

I made other home blunders like that from time to time. Like the time I decided to tighten the timing chain on my motorbike using the tensioner. As a sometimes reckless teenager my motto was 'if all else fails, read the instructions'. I undid and took off a nut on the bike engine that looked like it was part of the tensioner. As I took it off the bolt thread that was sticking out of the engine, that the nut was screwed onto, shot into the engine and disappeared. I then looked in the manual and it said loosen the nut then tighten it again – a spring would automatically take up the tension. It also said 'take care not to remove the nut or the tensioner bolt will disappear into the engine and you will have to take the engine out of the bike to fix it'. It takes quite a few of these blunders to really get the message, but we all get there in the end.

One domestic blunder still makes me laugh. This was my Dad down the garage car maintenance pit repairing his handbrake. Having made the repair he needed to test it by pulling on the handbrake and watching the mechanism, but he couldn't do that himself as he would have to climb out of the pit and then couldn't go back down and roll the car back over. At that moment my little sister ran past the garage so he called to her to come and pull on the handbrake while he watched the mechanism. She was glad to help and jumped into the car, but nothing was happening, despite lots of grunting. Eventually he said thanks and let her get back to the important business of play. He then climbed out of the pit and into the car to discover the indicator lever had been bent right around the steering column. Another important lesson learned there – always give proper training.

In my early days as a craft apprentice I spent some memorable time with excellent skilled mechanics in the surface fitting shop of the mine. After a while there I earned myself the nickname – 'Pigpen', as in one of Charlie Brown's friends in the cartoon. He was the one who always looked scruffy and had fleas buzzing all around him. It wasn't a reflection on my hygiene but the fact that at the end of any day's work I always seemed to be twice as mucky as anyone I worked with. I think the problem was I kind of abandoned myself to the dirt and grime of whatever we were doing and didn't worry much about it. In fact I hardly thought about it at all. That would sometimes mean if I had to scratch my cheek or my nose I would just go ahead, not realising my face was getting rather mucky. I guess I treated it like the Rugby field where you have to dive in and embrace the dirt rather than always trying to avoid it.

What particularly highlighted that aspect of my work was when I was deployed by the fitting shop gaffer to work with two of a team of three mechanics where the team leader was known for never getting a single dirty mark on him. That led to the inevitable questions from his competing peers as to whether he ever did any work at all. This was a criticism that I think partly arose as a reaction to the air of superiority he carried that led them to refer to his team as 'The King and I and the Court Jester'. In all fairness this guy and his team got through as much work as the best of them but he was just more dirt conscious than they were, and a whole lot more than I was.

One blunder I look back on, and still chuckle at from time to time, came when working with this particular team. As an apprentice I was assigned to their charge and we were sent to repair a pump at the bottom of the Coal Prep Plant. The pump had a massive inlet pipe about a metre in diameter that went level for a metre or two and then turned upwards disappearing up into the plant. The lead mechanic had loosened a flange connecting the pipe to the pump and then decided to give me the job of fully disconnecting it while he did something else at the rear of the pump. As he told me to do the job he hit the flange he had loosened with his huge spanner, but as he did so I saw a little fountain of thick slurry spurt out near to where he hit it. It took a minute or so for me to think about that. Slurry of that thickness would require quite a pressure to make even a little spurt like that. I then told the mechanic I wouldn't take the flange off because that pipe was clearly full of slurry and under pressure, after all who knows how high it goes. That was not the normal kind of refusal I would make as I would normally be up for most jobs, but on this occasion I unexplainably felt quite sure of myself. He was more than a little annoyed by my refusal but decided to let me do his job at the back of the pump while he took the flange off. Then, a few minutes later as I was at the back of the pump doing my job there was suddenly a massive gushing noise and a sudden flow of slurry swept past my feet up to the ankles of my boot. The mechanic came running out of there like a bat out of hell with his whole front, including his face, plastered with slurry, and the whole of his back still clean bright orange overalls. The pipe had burst apart and the slurry had hit him like a wall. All I could see was his eyes that he had cleared with two fingers as he came running out of there. In hindsight he was lucky – he could have been hurt. When he finally calmed down from the shock he headed off to the pit baths to change his overalls – and underpants too probably. His only real injury was his pride, especially given his reputation for cleanliness. It took me all my effort to stifle my laughter at the sight and memory of it but I decided to spare him further embarrassment by not telling any of his fellow mechanics in the surface fitting shop about it. If I had told them I doubt he would ever have forgiven me. He didn't thank me for my consideration there but I am pretty sure he was thankful and very relieved given the competitive nature of the fitting shop at that time. I doubt they would have ever let him forget it.

Of course the blunders I speak of are the unusual memorable things, not the norm. Most of the time the jobs for a mechanic hit snags and hitches, but these are normal and in the end the job gets done. However there is not much fun in reviewing all that routine stuff even though it is the majority of the work. The blunders you make, and the blunders of others you encountered are usually spread out over time, but the more you do the more you experience them and all these become fixed memories in your mind and stories to be shared at the appropriate time, as I am now doing of course.

With that disclaimer I come to one of the most embarrassing blunders I ever made, which was not at the mine but in my life after mining when I became a software developer. That is no excuse of course. By this time I was an experienced mechanic so I really should have known better, but the story is worth telling so I had to include it. It came after I had left mining and developed a software product that by this time had begun to sell around the world. One summer's day, with the sun shining outside I began to feel the need for more time doing the physical things I loved. I then had an epiphany. I suddenly began to question why I was working 9 to 5 every day and missing the glorious weather when my customers were spread around the globe and only ever contacted me by email. It didn't make sense. I was stuck in a work pattern that had no good reason for it. This was a particularly good summer with lots of nice warm weather. It was then I made a lifestyle change. I decided to kayak all the rivers in the North Nottinghamshire area. From there on for the whole summer I headed out on a kayaking adventure every other day. I realised how it could be done on my own. I would throw an old bike in the back of the car and tie the kayak to the roof of the car. I would then head downstream of

one of the rivers and drop the bike off, hiding it in the
nettles. I then headed upstream, parked the car and
dropped the kayak off. From there I rode down the river in
the kayak to the bike; rode the bike back to the car; and
then drove the car downstream to pick up the kayak.
Having collected both the bike and the kayak I would head
home arriving about 4pm. Then take a kip for an hour, and
then work from 5pm to midnight. It was the perfect life for
that whole summer.

Now, getting back to the story of the blunder I made. One
day I tied the kayak to the roof of the car using a rope I
thought would be perfectly adequate but unfortunately it
was the kind of plastic coated rope that is used for washing
lines and in truth it is really very weak. This particular day
I was driving back from one of my kayaking expeditions. I
had gathered some speed and was driving against the wind
down a slight incline with the kayak on my roof, when
suddenly the rope snapped. The kayak slid off the back of
the car and into the opposite carriageway, sliding along the
road. I immediately braked the car, but as it was an incline,
and fibre glass slips quite well on tarmac, the kayak began
to slide past me in the opposite carriageway alongside me.
It was one of those surreal moments that happen from time
to time that seems so unreal your brain begins to question
if this is really happening. Here I am racing my own kayak
that seems to have a mind and will of its own, along a
public road. Then I realised there was a car coming in the
other direction, and there was absolutely nothing I could
do about it. For a while the car just seemed to keep
coming, and then suddenly reacted by braking. By this
time the kayak was ahead of me, still in the opposite
carriageway. It was slowing rapidly, but not rapidly
enough. The car came to a halt but the kayak couldn't stop
in time – it jammed itself right under the front of the other
car. For a few brief moments nothing seemed to happen,

except perhaps I tried to snap out of the dream. Then the driver jumped out of the car. I decided I had to go and take the blame and assess the damage as apologetically as possible. As I met the driver he was distraught and began to pour out his tale of woe. He told me the car was brand new – only weeks old, and he had had two accidents in it already that were not his fault – something the insurance company were finding hard to believe, and now 'HE HAD HIT A CANOE'. As you may have gathered from my past, stifling laughter is something I had learned over the years but on this occasion I felt it was essential to maintain a serious and penitent expression.

The guy was actually quite distraught; I guess we all would have been with the same story. In the end the kayak had only damaged an underside panel for which I made a temporary repair and then later paid him cash of £300 for the proper repairs at a garage, so we kept the insurance companies out of it – they probably wouldn't have believed him anyway. It was the least I could do to say sorry and in the end we became friends and we both had a laugh about it. To be honest the money was worth it in the end because it gave me a great tale to tell at dinner parties. After all, what's life if it all goes smoothly with no problems or challenges? Of course I learned the lesson but still feel as an engineer it was a rooky mistake I never should have made, so I guess this is my confession for which I hope you, my dear reader, will grant me absolution.

CHAPTER 22

As mine roadways expand into new areas it is normal for them to be worked for a number of years, or even decades, until the coal reserves are worked out. Then the roadways are closed off and sealed because if they were all to be kept open they would require ventilation that in the end would become an overburden for the colliery's main fans such that other places would not get essential ventilation. Regulations would not allow roadways to remain open that were not properly ventilated as they could threaten the life of anyone that entered them due to the potential for a build-up of noxious gases that would poison or suffocate, or methane that could explode.

The mining health and safety regulations largely stemmed from the UK history of mining disasters where mines exploded through the ignition of methane, or later through the ignition of coal dust that would cause an explosion many times more powerful. A methane explosion could blow coal dust into the air and then trigger a coal dust explosion that would be many times more devastating. The worst mining disaster ever in the UK was a mine at Senghenydd, Wales that killed 439 miners with an explosion of this kind. The army now have a conventional weapon they call MOAB, which stands for 'Mother Of All Bombs' because it has explosive power that is as near as conventional weaponry gets to a nuclear explosion. It works by filling the air with explosive petroleum fumes and then igniting the whole cloud in one go. The huge mixture of oxygen and fuel produces a massive explosion. A coal dust explosion works on a very similar principle where the coal dust carries huge explosive energy and it is blown into a cloud where it is mixed with oxygen from the atmosphere that ignites and explodes.

The stories of such explosions from the past are an eternal memory and source of grief for those villages that lost large numbers of men from a whole generation where these explosions occurred. Many safety regulations have since been put in place to mitigate the danger, including dust suppression using water sprays, but also the distribution of stone dust in the roadways and on flimsy shelf like structures in the roadways. When the stone dust is blown into the air by an explosion it has the effect of stifling and damping a coal dust explosion so it gets no further than these 'stone dust barriers'.

There is one horror story I heard, which I believe is true, that really impacted me of an explosion at a UK mine many decades ago before these regulations were put in place. Both the police and the Mines Rescue Service were called to the scene of the explosion as the rapid response unit to help the miners below, if possible. The Mines Rescue Service existed precisely for this purpose. They were to be the first to enter the mine when a major incident occurred. I remember passing the Mines Rescue Centre for my area every day on my way to college at Mansfield. It was one place I never got to visit in my time in the industry. It had the look of a large fire station with vehicles clearly at the ready for any emergency, though some of the vehicles I saw that came from there were actually so old they had crash gears and no clutch, incredibly. I once rode in such a vehicle and saw the driver jamming the huge gear lever into gear knowing that if he failed it would have a kickback that would nearly break his arm. In my time I was never aware of the Mines Rescue being called out for a real emergency because by this time the safety measures had come to prevent that level of disaster, but the possibility that it would be needed still existed and the regulations demanded the service was provided. The horror story I heard was of a disaster where the police arrived first at a mine that had exploded and was on fire, so it was filled with smoke and fumes. Mines Rescue had breathing equipment and arrived ready to enter the mine despite the fact it would have had near zero visibility and would be extremely dangerous. The police judged the situation to be too dangerous and took the unprecedented step of preventing the Mines Rescue experts from entering the mine in order to prevent further loss of life. As word of the disaster spread the local villagers had rushed to the mine; wives desperate to see if their husbands were still alive or could be saved. When the police prevented the Mines Rescue Service from entering the mine to do their job their relatives became hostile towards the police. When the disaster passed, with many miners lost, that hostility deepened and in the next few months after the disaster two policemen were captured, kidnapped, and castrated by the bereaved wives and relatives that were bitter at them. After that the police on the beat had to be vigilant and always operate in pairs. This is a chilling story but it gives us a window into the kind of people mining communities could be in days gone by if they felt wronged or had some sense of grievance or injustice.

CHAPTER 23

Getting back to the problems of adequate ventilation; the air flow through the mine had to be carefully planned to be efficient – enough to cover all areas that remain open. Where the mine had multiple levels, all open at the same time, planning the layout of the mine could be challenging. It had to be decided which roadways were to provide an air intake through which air would flow to the coalfaces, and which would be the 'return' carrying exhaust air on its way back to the return shaft and the surface through the fans that were drawing it through the mine. By the time this air was exhaled from the mine by the fans it would be quite a cocktail or heat, dust and noxious or explosive gases. Often that led to really low quality of the air around mines where the dust would hang in the atmosphere, which was one reason for sometimes building mining housing estates about half a mile from the mine.

When planning that airflow layout of the mine, air doors would be strategically placed separating intake and return. They tended to be noisy places due to the leakage of air as some of it short circuited through gaps. Also both men and material, which often meant rail traffic, had to pass through these door, so they were constructed in banks of two, like a submarine hatch, that would mean one was sealed all of the time. Opening both doors would be a real misdemeanour unless you had specific permission for a brief moment or two for some special purpose. It would of course have the effect of starving parts of the mine of its air flow. If ever you were 'inbye' at the coalface and you felt the air stop flowing for any significant length of time you would begin to think about exiting the mine. It was something that rarely happened, even if the main fan broke down because there was always a backup fan to take over.

Mansfield Crown Farm Colliery, where for a while I was acting Shift Charge Engineer, had five levels all active at the same time. To maintain the air flow through all these workings certain roadways became vital to be kept open. This included an area that was deeper than any other part of the mine and where very few people ever went other than a pit Deputy once a week for the legal inspections, and sometimes technical staff to maintain the one piece of equipment that lived down there – a pump that pumped out mine water and kept the roadway open, including its electrical supply of course.

The roadway galleries there were the most eerie place I ever remember in a mine. Everything in it seemed untouched from the 1950s. You could find a newspaper tucked away in the wall cavities that was from 1955 and read the news from back then. It had the sense of it having seen real action many decades ago but now it had just an eerie stillness with the faint echo of men from the past that worked and lived their lives there. Inevitably rumours of haunting in these galleries spread around the mine, especially after one of the Deputies 'swore blind' to some very weird and scary paranormal activity down there. My personal sense of the place was that it was very interesting, and very peaceful, like a museum, and always a good place to visit for the experience. However, suspicion is more of a feature for some men, even miners, and wild horses wouldn't drag some of them there after those rumours. After all, everyone knew that men had died in the mines, especially in days gone by. It seemed all too feasible for it to be haunted. Was it true? Well, if you want my personal opinion I think it was a deliberate rumour started by a Deputy who liked to go there as the official, because it was peaceful, pleasant and quiet, and his stories served to make others reluctant to challenge him for the job, so he kept it for himself. Sometimes the truth is as simple as that. But who knows for sure?

One of my most challenging times at the pit came while I was covering the night shift and the pump in these same galleries broke down. The pump lived in a sump, which is a part of the roadway shaped like the U-bend of a toilet, and the bottom of the sump was the very lowest point of the mine. The area was so remote that even getting a pump there was a challenging task as there were no easy means of transport. It required a lot of muscle, manpower and effort – much like the old slaves that built the pyramids. When the pump broke down and proved unrepairable we realised our oversight that there was no spare pump on site ready to replace it. Normally that would not be such a disaster, but what transpired was that if this roadway was closed off it would starve many vital parts of the mine of ventilation and actually put the mine under threat because the water would rise to the point where it would cut the roadway off completely. Then the problem of accessing the far side of the sump where the pump was would become even worse, through unventilated roads, as it would mean traversing many miles of nearly inaccessible roadway to get there. Transporting heavy equipment via those routes would be a massive challenge. In desperation the problem forced us to try to get the old pump working again, even if temporarily – enough to give some time to the men that were transporting the new equipment to do the job.

By this time the roadway had filled considerably with mine water and was reduced to a few feet of open roadway near the roof where the air was whistling though at a hurricane pace. It was then that I needed two fitters to get to the pump with some new spares that had just arrived to try to fix it. They had to get there as quickly as possible, but that was now difficult given the path they had to take. Then one of my fitters made a suggestion that hadn't even occurred to me – 'we will go through the water'. I hadn't even considered that. The problem is mine water is quite acidic and not the kind of water you would want to be dipping into. Nevertheless this fitter and his mate were keen for the challenge – I think they had a real sense of adventure and knew there were bragging rights up for grabs if they pulled it off. It would be a bit of a James Bond type adventure. I explained that the water acidity would be a problem but they had an answer for everything, which was 'we with get lathered up with the barrier cream used in the surface fitting shop before we go'. My answer was still no. I didn't like the sound of it, but at the same time I was desperate, and so in fact was the whole mine.

It was then someone else made another suggestion – 'take the dingy'. My first reaction was to laugh, but I then realised the guy who suggested it was serious, so I said, 'what dingy?' I had never heard of 'the dingy'. It just didn't seem to be the kind of equipment you see at a mine. He then told me there was a dingy in the colliery stores that was there for just such an eventuality as this. That fact suddenly changed things. It changed from me being responsible for two foolhardy fitters taking a risk to save the mine by wallowing in mine water, to me opening myself up for criticism for not taking the one option that they had already prepared for of sending the dingy into the mine. The fitters were still up for it, so rightly or wrongly, I made a decision. I got the dingy from the stores and deployed the men to do the job with it.

They were gone for most of the shift and out of range of telephone communication so I didn't know what was happening. That is often the case for us charge hands – we simply rely on the heroism of those we command. In the end these men arrived back in my office having left the dingy on site. They had tried to sail the boat through the gap that was left near the roof of the U-bend, against the howling prevailing wind whistling through. The gap was even tighter now and the boat didn't fit through, but in their zeal and determination to succeed these two guys had got into the water and swam through the gap to the other side. They then fixed the pump, which itself was an accomplishment, and with the pump now working they made their way back the same way. When they finally reached my office they stripped off their top layer of clothing to reveal skin that was bright red all over having dipped into the acidic mine water, but they were in very high spirits having succeeded in their missions and I sensed they could hardly wait to claim the bragging rights in the Welfare that evening over a drink where they could tell their mates and their family their tales of bravado. For me they deserved it all. I don't think I would have deployed them had I known just what it would take, but sometimes it really does work out if you give someone a challenge to be the actual hero instead of sitting on a couch and watching it faked on TV all the time.

CHAPTER 24

Occasionally you would come across stories of something really ridiculous that someone had done that would thereafter become part of their legacy that they would find hard to live down. For example there was the day a guy walked into the surface fitting shop of the mine with his hands carefully held at certain distance apart and said to the first worker he met he needed a piece of steel this length. There was a procedure for requests for materials, and that required a drawing and description, including material sizes and dimensions, but not everybody understood this. What made this case legendary was that the guy in question had made his hand measurement in the pit bottom, and then travelled up the shaft in the cage and walked about 200 metres across the pit yard, still with his hands held apart, believing he had not moved his hands at all before delivering his request. There were times when you would accommodate an unofficial request to keep a job going, but this went beyond the bounds of credibility and earned the guy a fair share of ridicule thereafter.

When it came to mechanics there were various classifications – class 1, class 2, conveyor belt and rope haulage fitters, chock fitters, unqualified labourers. This classification was generally tied to their academic achievements, but some of them couldn't spell academic, let alone pass the exams, so they were given a lower rank and assigned the kind of jobs that would fit their skillset. However, academic achievement was not always the whole story with these guys. They could still be very wily, creative individuals that survived by their wits, despite their inability to handle the academic learning. For example I once managed a team that had only class 2 mechanics and they had a steelwork problem of two measurements making up the two sides of a right-angled triangle and they needed the measurement of the diagonal – meaning the hypotenuse to those of us that did maths at school. I decided to hold back and see what they made of the problem. Their solution was to draw it out in chalk on the fitting shop floor and then measure the result. I couldn't fault their ingenuity. It was their way of solving the problem and it worked perfectly for their purposes. When I mentioned Pythagoras and his theorem they thought I was talking Greek, which of course I was. They found the idea of a maths solution hard to believe and challenged me to a race to find the answer. I had the disadvantage of having to work out a square root without a calculator so that slowed me a little bit and the race was quite close, but I did manage to pip them to the post, which made my point and maybe made them a little more appreciative of the academic skills some of their colleagues had worked so hard to achieve. For some of these guys even the idea of a scale drawing would be a problem so they would be forced to do their working out full size. In some cases that may mean quite an area of floor space, but then if that is what you have to do to get the job done, then that is what you have to do. For some of them the alternative of asking an academic was just not going to happen so that would be their only option to save face in those circumstances.

Despite the disdain of some, academic skills often helped a lot. Take for example the day a coalface broke down because one of the two electric motors driving the steel face conveyor, the panzer, had failed. The face and all the men were stood still at the potential cost of hundreds of thousands of pounds. When I inquired about the size of motors on the conveyor they told me 200 horse power. This meant the face had been upgraded from the usual 150 horse power motors. Nobody seemed to appreciate the implications of that. The conveyor needed 150 horse power to run empty. That meant one 200 horse power motor could drive the conveyor alone with 50 horse power left spare to carry coal. That was the main purpose for upgrading the motors in the first place, but sometimes those messages just don't get through. Once they discovered it the face was back in production in a jiffy running on the one motor, which cut the losses considerably. These are the times a bit of academic knowledge comes in really handy.

Then there was the time we began to get new machines in the mine that the department I was in charge of were responsible for, known as FSVs, or Free Steered Vehicles. This was a move away from the caterpillar tracked vehicles we had always had, like tanks tracks, to six-wheeled rubber tired vehicles that were like a huge insects with an articulated joint in the middle. These were much more versatile vehicles, useful in many ways that the tracked vehicles were not, but no sooner had we got them than we began to have loads of problems of conveyors getting wrecked somewhere along the roadways, which sometimes halted production at considerable cost and led to the belt fitters becoming decidedly overworked and angry. At times the FSV drivers would deny blame to the last, trying to avoid the consequences, but it was clearly them that were causing the problem. Then I caught one of them get into difficulties in an enclosed space where there was a conveyor and I saw the driver trying to get out of it without wrecking anything. Everything he did seemed to make the problem worse with this articulated vehicle and as he tried to escape the machine gradually moved more and more into the conveyor threatening to permanently damage it. It was one of those moments that required us as mechanics to stop and think through the problem. Even though the drivers had been through the manufacturers training on driving these vehicle they hadn't been given the information on how to get out of a jam like this. I realised the problem was with the centre of the machine moving over, so in the end we got the driver to drop his hydraulic bucket at the front onto wooden nogs that lifted the machine up, then use thc steering to turn the vehicle which slewed the middle of the machine across with the middle wheels skidding sideways on the ground, rather that slewing one end of the vehicle as normal. Then we raised the bucket so the wheels were all lowered back to the ground and the problem was solved, the driver was out of trouble and could do the rest easily. This was a really counterintuitive solution that not even the vehicle manufacturers had thought of, but once we discovered it and just one single driver had seen it, word spread almost immediately to all the other drivers and we never had another problem of wrecked conveyors. Sometimes a little bit of thought and knowledge can solve a real problem that in turn saves a lot of money through preventing lost production.

Another case I remember like this was a bit more financially costly to the mine in question. Each pit would have some kind of underground bunker to store and buffer coal ready for loading onto the 'skip' which is like a cage in the return air mine shaft but designed to carry coal rather than men. The bunker in one mine consisted of metal conveyors, like the face panzer, carrying a bed of coal and rock, and it would occasionally seize up from the weight of coal and stone in the bunker which meant the whole mine would be at a standstill, at huge cost, until it was fixed. Then someone decided on a solution to install plates at each side of the bunker to carry some of the weight of the coal. At great expense the modifications were made during the downtime in the pit holidays. When the bunker started up again not only was the problem not solved, it was worse. For some reason the plates restricted the flow of coal even more and jammed the conveyors more than before they were installed.

The reason for the problem was that when you take a bed of mineral like this and agitate it, even though the mineral is a solid it behaves just like a fluid, and is termed in academia as a 'fluidised bed'. That meant the mineral would develop the same kind of pressure above and below the plates in the same way that it would if it were water or some other fluid of the same density. All the plates did was to cause more drag. On this occasion it was the lack of this bit of understanding that meant these modifications were a huge expensive experiment that was doomed to fail. The managers were forced to close the mine and strip the modification out as quickly as possible to cut the losses. Sometimes these mistakes just have to happen for the learning curve to continue, and no doubt at times the same mistake got repeated from pit to pit, though we would hope the area headquarters would do their best to prevent it. After all, the solution in this case seemed perfectly logical, but the real result was a bit counterintuitive so we ended up paying the cost of the mistake – quite a high one in this case due to lost production. Of course it is easy to criticise mistakes like this in hindsight, but at times to make progress you often have to do so by taking two steps forward and one step back. Of course as technicians we always tried to minimise these errors but the nature of the game of mining meant there would always be problems to solve, and mistakes would be made that we would later wish to forget about.

I did make my own mistakes though. Some at the pit and some domestic. I remember one day when my cold water tank finally rusted through after 50 years and sprang a leak in my house, I decided there wasn't any good reason for having a cold water tank in the first place as all it did was feed water to the hot water tank, so why not cut out the middle man and couple the mains directly to the hot water tank, at least until I had a new cold water tank to install. This I did and discovered the whole reason for it when the mains water pressure blew the top of my hot water tank, so I had to replace that as well. That was on the same week we were studying something called 'hoop stress' at university, which basically tells you if you couple the mains to something as big as a hot water tank it will blow the top off it. It's a pity we hadn't done that item of the curriculum the week before, it would have saved me a lot of time and expense. They say a little knowledge can be a dangerous thing. Sometimes a smartass ends up getting his ass kicked.

Another case I remember well at the pit was a job I requested to be assigned to so I could see it because it would be a huge task and quite a rare opportunity. That was a considerable modification to the coal winder at Clipstone Colliery that would alter the single rope winder to a twin rope winder. Clipstone was distinguished as the highest pit headstocks in Europe, which was a necessary thing because it was a very deep mine of just over 1000 yards and it had a 'Koepe' friction winder. That simply meant that rather than winding up a coil of rope – meaning a steel rope of more than 4 inches diameter – the rope would wind over several huge pulleys in the headstocks that would grip it by friction, but it would not coil it up like other winding engines do, it would simply go over the pulley and back down the mineshaft on the other side. The height of the headstocks was necessary to make the rope wind onto the pulleys enough to give it the right amount of friction grip. That friction idea solved the problem of trying to coil up a huge length of rope for such a deep mine. The reason for the modification was to try to solve the problem of the coal skip twisting and rotating in the shaft as the rope effectively uncoiled a bit under the strain of a coal load. The job would take Area Headquarters something like a full year to plan the job and it would require the labour of many men during the pit holidays to accomplish it. In the end the long and the short of it is it made no difference and didn't solve the problem.

I can't make it out from the online photographs but if you look closely at the headstock that is enclosed at Clipstone the huge winding wheel there should have two rope grooves in it rather than one where the twin ropes sat.

The pit headstocks at Clipstone are the only ones in Nottinghamshire still standing, and in my view they are a thing of real beauty. Not all would agree, I know, but I understand why the locals opted to keep them as a feature of the legacy of the village; they are magnificent. For me the towers are monuments that are a really impressive eyeful putting the village of Clipstone on a par with the city of Paris and that famous guy also called Eiffel.

CHAPTER 25

Coming back to the mechanics and fitters I had to manage; what mattered most to me and the other shift charge engineers, even more than intelligence, was the self-discipline of the men that made them really hard workers. If they lacked knowledge we could always form teams to compensate for that, or give them training. But if they didn't have the discipline of work then that could be a real problem, especially when it came to handling production critical repairs and maintenance during breakdowns or at times when the mine was at a standstill during weekends or holidays and work had to be completed ready for the restart. From that point of view one of the best workers I ever had was a guy by the name of Chuck who was a coalface hydraulic chock fitter.

Chuck the chock fitter is quite a cute name and it fit him exactly as a person. He was the kind of amiable, likable Postman Pat type of guy you sometimes meet. He was quite a small guy, with bottle bottom glasses, and so friendly he didn't have an aggressive bone in his body. He just took all the flack and banter he got in his stride. I guess he was just used to all that having had it all his life. He was also an incredibly hard worker, and everyone knew it, which earned him a great deal of respect at the pit despite the fact he was a funny little chap. His job was to maintain the chocks on the coalface. Each face would have about 200 hydraulic chocks along with all the supporting equipment such as high pressure pumps and miles and miles of hoses connecting them all up. The technical level wasn't as high as some of the machinery we worked with, but it was technical enough with all the hydraulic valves and other equipment that could be quite complex, as hydraulics can be. Chuck the chock fitter knew his job inside out and would work all shift, sometimes not even breaking to eat if the job demanded it. You just knew if he spent any length of time on a coalface it would soon be in ship shape so breakdowns became far less likely. Nobody knows what kind of money he saved the mine through his work by avoiding downtime and production losses through breakdowns, but my guess is it was considerable.

Sometimes the guys that worked with Chuck felt overworked trying to keep up. I remember one such guy telling me he desperately needed a break from work and so he took time off and booked an exotic, romantic holiday to Rome with his partner hoping to get away from it all. When he got to Rome there they were walking through the city and they came across a fountain, and there to his horror sitting on the side of the fountain was Chuck the chock fitter, still apparently wearing his grey vest that he always wore down the pit. After hoping for a complete break from mining in Nottinghamshire, this was quite a shock and disappointment, but he gathered himself and walked over to Chuck to say hello, who just looked at him with no hint of surprise and just said 'Bloody hot I'nit' – the very same thing he would always say when you bumped into him down the pit. What are the odds? No doubt Chuck was missing the pit, having had to finally take his holidays or lose them, and for him meeting his workmate was probably quite a welcome coincidence.

Of course when Chuck was away or on another shift the work had to go on, but we would really miss him. At times you had to depend on others, like that team we called 'Rigour and Mortis' I mentioned earlier. These guys were the very antithesis of Chuck. Their main skill was to write reports that convinced you they had worked their butt off all shift when in truth they had probably done less than an hour of work and spent the remainder of the their time lounging around, or sitting on their haunches. I once showed Chuck one of their reports from the previous night shift where the two of them had installed a total of two chock leg protectors. If these were the high quality type it meant they had to lower off the hydraulic chock legs to install them and that would require a bit of work, though not enough for a whole shift for even one of them. When I showed Chuck the report he explained these weren't the high quality ones; they were the type that just wrapped around the leg which meant they took less than ten minutes to install, but the report was written like it was slave labour for the whole shift.

Most of the time the shift charge engineers would just deploy these guys out of the way so nothing critical depended on them, but that of course just made the problem worse, and it could be quite demoralising for the other fitters because they knew they were carrying the work load of these bone idlers. At times I saw shift charge engineers challenge them and try to get them to work, but that would start a political battle that took a whole lot of energy – energy that none of us had spare when we were trying to handle everything else that was going on at the mine at the same time. These guys had a way of turning any demand for them to actually do some work into accusations against the engineer for not supplying the tools, or the equipment, or something that was essential to the job. In the case of Chuck he always took responsibility for that and made sure he had what he needed, as did most. By contrast, unless you put everything directly into the hands of these guys they would claim to be unable to do the job for reasons that were never their fault.

For these particular guys I never got the chance to challenge them because I was moved to take charge of another department managing the installation and maintenance of the road heading machines at the pit. These were perhaps the most complex machines we had. Most of them were the tank like tracked machines with cutting booms for cutting roadways. There were 35 of them in all at this pit weighing up to 87 tonnes. For that job I needed competent staff and I was lucky to have the men I needed, but there were times when I was in charge of the whole shift that I had to challenge some that would pull the standard down if we let them.

For example there were ones that would refuse to be deployed to certain parts of the mine, or to do certain jobs, and in that way they tried to secure easier work so others had to carry the load. Any hint of that meant I would instantly deploy them to those places and jobs. In the end they chose to handle it by coming to an agreement with their work colleagues on who would do what, and that was ok by me, but if I showed favouritism to one just to keep the peace it would not help me to maintain the commitment and respect of the others, so it would make my job much harder.

The same went for the young apprentice that felt he could turn up late and then do what he wanted because he was the relative of one of the high ranking managers at the mine. When I sent him home he was shocked having never had that treatment before, but the rest of the men appreciated the justice of the move and their respect always seemed to come back in dividends with their willingness to work hard and do their best for me and the team. Fortunately the apprentice took the hint and I heard through the grapevine his manager relative was actually quite pleased I had done it, even though he wouldn't say that to me directly.

I found some of the most hardworking teams on my staff were conveyor belt fitters and the haulage rope men. I would be skilled and able enough to do pretty much any practical job of my staff at the pit if I had to, having trained in all departments. The one big exception to that was a very highly skilled job – the job of the rope men. They were responsibly for splicing steel ropes together without reducing the strength of the ropes because that could lead to breakage which could be extremely dangerous, especially where the haulage went down a drift (an incline) as it frequently did. Splicing ropes would often take whole shifts, or even whole weekends, and they were usually quite production critical because the whole supply chain for the coalface would depend on them. I therefore gave the rope men respect, and plenty of rope, so to speak. Between breakdowns they would have some much quieter times, which was just how the job worked. All we needed to know was that they were ready to spring into action if a breakdown occurred or when they were needed. There were times on the afternoon shift that exactly that would happen and I would suddenly need them, but nobody seemed to know where they were and I was unable to contact them. It was then – when they seemed to have disappeared off the face of the earth that I knew exactly where to look. There was a large pond on the pit top where someone had decided to use it to unofficially breed carp. When the rope men disappeared you could guarantee they would be there feeding the fish. That's one good about fishermen – you just know where to look to find them. On afternoons they would sneak up the pit early for a bit of fish time, but we didn't mind that as long as we knew we could find them and they would spring into action when we really needed it.

CHAPTER 26

One thing that mining inevitably develops is a whole jargon of its own, apart from all the accents you hear, to the point that when you first hear it there are so many words you don't understand it sounds like a foreign language. At first all you can do is listen like a dog to its master hoping to hear a word you recognise like 'here Henry', or 'who's a good boy then'. Like any new environment, as you spend more time there you quickly climb the learning curve until the words that once seemed so foreign seem perfectly natural and logical. You then wonder why others who are new to mining look so confused when you try to communicate with them. That was brought home to me one day when a lady secretary in the offices at a mine asked me if I would explain something to her. She then showed me a memo she had been given to type up. She pointed out a sentence, as an example, that described the task of attaching coffins to a dog kennel. It seemed perfectly logical to me but for her she was wondering if someone was having a big joke and was winding her up, or if not then what the hell was going on down that mine! When I realised how it looked to her I had to take a break to stop laughing, which confirmed to her it must be a joke. When I calmed down I was able to assure her there were no dogs down the mine, nor were there any burials going on. I explained the dog kennels house the electric motors on the face conveyor and they are dog kennel shaped, and the coffins are steel containers with lids that carry the cables along the face and protect them from damage. In my world of mining, coffins attached to dog kennels was perfectly normal and logical, but having thought about it I perfectly understand her concern and dilemma there and was able to assure her there really was no need for her to call either the police or the RSPCA after all.

I wrote earlier about the many 'interesting' characters you meet in mining. By far the most extreme of those could be found in the mining department, rather than the technical departments. Many miners were intelligent, amiable, law abiding citizens, even if somewhat rough and ready, but there were always some that to describe them as 'a loose cannon' would really understate the matter. Then if they were the kind that were said to be 'not the sharpest tool in the box', so to speak, you had to be prepared for the unpredictable, and at times the downright unbelievable.

One such case I remember hearing about at another mine was of two brothers who took the opportunity to nick some explosives from the mine. Normally explosives are carefully checked out and checked in from the special stores on the pit surface, along with detonators and other equipment needed to use them, but there are always ways for men to try to deceive the Deputy in charge and somehow get access to these explosives. Of course if caught it would mean instant sack, but if a Deputy did lose a stick of explosive it could become a huge political issue and a blot on his record. Therefore there were times when a stick or two went missing and the Deputy decided to hush it up rather than face the music. It would also be easy for him to question his own actions and think that he had made a mistake of putting more explosives into one of the holes drilled for them than he intended. Of course there was no way to check the mistake once the explosion had been detonated. In some cases if a Deputy suspected foul play he would alert the 'banksmen' and 'onsetter' that manned the pit top and pit bottom. It was part of their duty to search men for contraband, such as smoking equipment, as they entered or exited the mine so if explosives went missing they would use their powers to search men to try to relocate them. However all the men would have to do is to stash the nicked explosives somewhere in the mine for a few days until things calmed down and then take them up the mine when the chances of being searched were low, especially at the end of a shift when the whole shift of men were keen to get up the mine, get bathed and go home.

In this case the two brothers in question had a plan to rob a bank using the nicked explosives – clearly after watching too many influential movies. As part of their preparation they decided to test it out by trying it on a now disused outside brick bog – i.e. a brick toilet, on the mining housing estate where they lived. This they did but it made such a loud bang it woke up the whole village and the police were called. The men were arrested and confessed their crimes and their intentions given that the options were to either admit to their criminal intentions, or be branded terrorists. They chose the former and to do their time as sentenced.

In hindsight the comedy value of these kind of stories is great, but also scary at the same time. After all, I did say before that mining is like war. You really had to be aware of just what power there is in an explosive to understand what a scary thought it is for guys of this calibre to get their hands on them. When explosives are set off in the mine, holes are first drilled deep into the rock, then the explosives are pushed deep inside and cemented in place. You then have to withdraw quite a distance along the roadways and wait for the explosion. The explosion would be damped hugely by the rock it was designed to blast so it would be like being hit by a huge semi firm pillow of air. That could be a little deceptive for people who decided to try it on a brick bog. Their chances of blowing themselves to pieces was very real.

To train the Deputies responsible for the explosives and give them an appreciation of the power involved they would be sent to a site near South Normanton in North Nottinghamshire where the explosives were manufactured, and there they would be given a demonstration of a 'slurry explosive' that would work underwater, by blowing up a small pond. When I did the training the trainers made us guess how high the blast would send the pond. Some guessed 30 feet, others 50 feet. We were at a distance looking down a hill to the pond for the demo. When it blew we were looking nearly vertically upwards at the fountain of water to a height of more than 300 feet. That was enough to give you some appreciation of just what kind of force and power you were dealing with. The men in charge of the demo were clearly people who found a whole lot of satisfaction in their job, with all their surprised visitors – perhaps a little too much for comfort I thought because they would then tell us a story, with great relish, of the day they were doing the demo and an unsuspecting duck flew in and landed on the pond. No prizes for guessing what happened next, though like the duck I'm not sure the onlookers were quite ready and expecting it on that occasion.

CHAPTER 27

After leaving mining I worked for one large company for a while where one of the contractual conditions of employment were, I quote: 'No horse play'. I had to think to myself how things change. Back in the mines horse play was almost an unofficial job qualification requirement, and much of the time that is part of the culture of the mines that makes miners really love to work there. To say no horse play to many of them is like saying don't breathe.

Yes the mines are tough, no question. But when the mines began to close I met miners who were literally in tears because the culture of mining was everything they had ever experienced, known or loved. Of course the job must be done, and that was the priority. But it was the comradery that meant so much to them and the constant banter and 'horse play' was a big part of it.

Of course the miners didn't have a monopoly on horse play. Whilst at college I had the chance to visit RAF Wittering where the Harrier jump jets and the Lightning jets were kept. There an engineer invited one of us to sit in the pilot seat of a Harrier. One guy leapt at the chance and so he got the job. Then as he was sitting in the pilot's seat the engineer began to tell us about the ejector seat, telling us that when it went off it was so powerful each ejection would permanently shorten the spine of the pilot by half an inch, and so any pilot that had ejected three times would no longer be eligible to fly the jet. Also if he hadn't fastened the straps around his legs an ejection would rip his knee caps off. He explained that if it went off in the hanger we were in it would shoot the pilot upwards by 300 feet, which would mean he would crash straight through the roof of the hanger with no chance of survival. The guy now sitting in the seat started to look a bit unnerved by that, but the engineer assured him that he was safe because there was a safety pin in the rip cord that we could see between his legs with the distinct warning colours of a yellow and black stripe, and that pin would stop the ejector seat from being triggered. Our guy looked relieved. Or at least he did until the engineer challenged him to remove the pin. Of course he was from mining stock like me and therefore had to comply to save face. Very nervously he slid the pin out of the rip cord lever as carefully as he could. Then, having removed it, and still looking a bit nervous there was suddenly a massive, loud bang. Our hearts stopped, and then raced as we tried to recover. The engineer had slapped the canopy as hard as he could and scared us half to death, at which he was rolling around laughing at us and especially at the guy in the seat. Apparently it was a standard joke for all visitors. Yep, as I was saying earlier, 'all is fair in love and war (and mining)', which seems to also include the British armed forces and any highly irresponsible horse play they can come up with.

One of the scrapes I have had or witnessed in the past came not in the mines but on holiday at Scarborough when a Lightning jet came over Scarborough Rock. The jet took a bird strike as it went over and was forced to ditch in the North Bay. I was on my way out to sea for a fishing trip from Scarborough harbour at the time so we saw the whole thing happen. We turned back towards the crash site but were sent on our way over the radio by the military who didn't want us to approach. The pilot was killed as he was flying so low he couldn't react fast enough and though he did eject he hit the tail of the plane on ejection. It is a very rare thing for it to happen, and an extremely rare thing to see it. I asked someone at RAF Wittering about the event who whispered to me 'Oh yes he shouldn't have been there. He got bollocked for that didn't he?' I said I thought he was killed. The guy said 'Yes, that's what I meant'. I always find there is a real rapport between people with occupations where they are constantly putting their lives on the line for their job.

CHAPTER 28

Sometimes the mistakes we make in life are the things that prepare us for handling dangerous situations in the future, if we survive it of course. Most of those mistakes come when we are children so to survive without pain we have to learn quickly.

One of my most memorable incidents came with my best friend Colin in secondary school. He was much smaller than me but really feisty and adventurous. In this particular misadventure we tied a tree swing on a favourite tree over the river Maun near Ollerton, but the rope was long and we didn't want to cut it. We wanted to save it for some much bigger swings in the forest. We decided instead to make two swings from the same branch with the spare rope – not the best idea we ever had. Then one could swing from the river bank across the river, while the other could launch from another branch and swing up and down the river. The fact that the trajectories of these swings crossed didn't seem to be problem as we didn't intend to use them both together, did we? I launched off the high swing from the branch when Colin suddenly had second thoughts about that. We met at high speed in the middle. I was seriously winded in the kidneys as I hit his head. Colin was catapulted into the water unconscious. He came around a bit as he hit the cold water and tried to swim. Still crippled myself, I managed to grab him despite the excruciating pain and drag him to the bank. After a while recovering we walked home but he was really dazed and I was bruised. Later his mum rang me to ask what had happened because Colin had slept a long time – he was concussed. When he came around he couldn't remember a single thing about it. Pain is real a teacher, if you remember it of course, but I think I must have had quite a short memory because I seemed to need a regular dose of it as a teenager to keep myself from another total wipe-out.

In actual fact I had a constant stream of adventures like that with my friends, too much to tell it all, but we survived. Having said that the era of 100mph, 250cc Japanese motorbikes came along where those bikes were legal for provisional rider. I had one myself. There were quite a number in that era that did get wiped out and didn't survive – many were killed, which is why they changed the law to max 125cc for provisional riders and introduced proper training. Colin broke his legs in the first week of owning one. That was his femur leg bones, the upper leg, which can be life threatening. He crashed in the same accident as another friend who damaged his bike but wasn't hurt, though no-one was killed in that case. Fortunately he recovered. I myself had two accidents over my time with a motorbike, and a brother had one on my bike. In mine I skidded to a stop on my leathers in one case, and in the other I ended up over a wall in someone's rose garden, and neither of those were my fault. In both cases I was avoiding drivers that were simply not bike aware. No doubt we all needed proper training to think on behalf of everyone else on the road as well as ourselves, and that basically became law after that era where many young guys got injured or killed.

CHAPTER 29

When I think about the whole operation of mining in my area it still impresses me even today. Not just the amazing surface installations with the iconic headstocks, or the hundreds of miles of underground roadways at many levels that I had seen for myself. But also the huge network of rail tracks with all the bridges and tunnels above ground to transport the coal we had won. No Thomas the Tank Engine fan could fail to appreciate the frequent sight I saw from the upper window of my house on the mining housing estate in Edwinstowe that looked out across the flood plain of the river Maun to the train track in the distance on the other side. There you would get a panoramic view of the full length of a huge diesel engine pulling a train of 30 wagons or more laden with coal from the collieries further up the line – Clipstone, Bilsthorpe, Rufford, Blidworth, Welbeck and Mansfield Crown Farm Collieries. From there it would head on east with its load, over the bridge in the middle of Edwinstowe near the Dukeries Hotel where I once saw steam trains as a child, then it would pick up the Thoresby branch line and go on to sneak under and over the roads of Ollerton, picking up Ollerton Colliery and the branch line to Bevecotes Colliery that passed through Boughton and through the quarter mile tunnel near Walesby Scout camp – a place I once was caught with a train coming and had to dive into a manhole while the train passed. From there it went on through the countryside past Kirton and through Tuxford until it eventually terminated near the west bank of the River Trent, a little south of Newark, at High Marnham power station. Of course the whole operation didn't stop there. The coal would then be pulverised and burnt using the heat to create steam that would drive the massive steam turbines, that generated the electrical energy, that came back to us to drive our electric kettles in the morning for a drink before we headed off to work at the pit, making it worth every bit of the effort we made to get the coal out of the ground in the end. Mining was never just a job, it was a way of life. Or to be more accurate, lots of ways of life for many different people doing many different jobs.

In actual fact at one time not all the coal these local mines produced went to the power station. Many of us still remember the Rexco petroleum plants near Ollerton and Thoresby Collieries where coal was processed to extract petroleum. Those plants disappeared before I arrived in the industry because cheaper petroleum could be obtained directly from other places like the North Sea, but for a while there was a demand for the higher quality coal that had a good petroleum content to serve them. That demand directly affected the seams that these collieries chose to mine because each seam has a different quality of coal and the petroleum content would vary for each one.

When the petroleum industry ended in the area there was some relief for a number of reasons. One was that it greatly affected the quality of air in the area. I was told by old time office workers at Thoresby Colliery that they would shut all the windows tightly over the weekend but on Monday morning there would be a thin film of oil over every surface in the offices that had all settled out of the air, all coming from the petroleum plant. Many of us were raised in that kind of environment and if evolution is true we may have adapted to some degree internally to have lungs that work something like an internal combustion engine.

The other effect of the petroleum plants closing was that the coal demand shifted exclusively to energy production and that required only lower grade quality coal. At Thoresby that led to a push for the deeper *Parkgate* seam at about 1000m depth; a seam which was more than two metres in height, rather than shallower coal seams like the *High Hazel* and the *Top Hard* at around a 1m to 1.5m height that were higher quality coal but lower seam depth.

For those that don't know it, all coal seams were given names like this, of which there are more than two hundred at different levels in most of the Nottinghamshire coalfield region, each with a unique quality of coal. Some of the names are fascinating and there is some real history to the naming of them, though many of the seams are very thin – some are just a few inches. The *Parkgate* seam was deep, but a high seam of relatively low quality coal, ideal for power stations which required a certain amount of ash in the product with low petroleum. At that time the other collieries in the area also made similar moves to win the same coal from these deeper, higher seams so the bonus was the raw tonnage production figures shot up. For Bevercotes to access the *Parkgate* seam they just sunk the shaft deeper as it could be done when the mine was developed. For an established pit like Thoresby the only feasible way was to drive down inclined roadways, which we called drifts that descended deeper into the mine by about another 250m or so. These too would be a major undertakings requiring massive investment, but the venture came to pay off well as there was an abundance of coal there and all the ground that had already been covered at a higher level could be covered again. The higher seam also meant the coalfaces were much easier places to work, especially for a tall guy like me, as you were able to stand up and even run down the face rather than crawl. I remember many shifts on the lower seams before they closed where I was forced to wear knee pads and crawl. If you were not calloused up and used to it then it would be purgatory on these faces as the knee pad straps would dig into the back of your knees all shift. These were the days before Velcro, which may have helped a bit had we had it, however, remarkably there were some guys that much preferred working these lower seams to the taller ones once they got used to those conditions where they were kneeling and crawling, sitting or lying down all day. I always found the lower seams much harder work.

CHAPTER 30

I said it before, mining is not just a job, it's a way of life, and it's a culture. In some ways that culture came from the fact it was a nationalised industry for so long. There wasn't much hire and fire going on as you find it in private industry, and the unions were strong enough to make a serious defence of any rough treatment from management which all served towards developing that particular culture where the power between men and management was in fact quite finely balanced.

An example of that was one day down the mine I decided to stay to help with a job that was happening on a dead shift of a coalface. The mines always tried to manage things in such a way that at least one face had a dead shift so then when there was a big problem on another face – maybe a breakdown, or a geological problem, managers had the option to deploy men to work the dead shift and so production would not be impacted. On this shift the face was dead, as planned, and it provided the opportunity for some much needed maintenance work to be done. That required a number of miners to dig the machinery out from the debris that had accumulated around it. This was welcome overtime for the men in question – they were always happy to earn a little extra money, usually to please the wife because as the saying goes 'happy wife, happy home'.

As the shift got started one of the men spotted a puddle of mine water in the roadway. He therefore did the usual thing and went to find a telephone, which on this occasion was quite nearby so I heard most of his conversation. The thing is, the rules stated that men were entitled to slightly higher hourly rates if they had to work in water or wet conditions, or if there was some unusual element of danger to their work. The puddle was therefore seen as a definite negotiating opportunity. For the next three quarters of an hour, while the other miners were waiting for him so they could get started on their overtime job, he spent arguing with the district Deputy, his line manager, as to whether the puddle in the roadway constituted wet conditions that qualified them for the extra money. The funny part was that he had to describe the conditions that were the basis of his claim so we all got to hear how far he dared exaggerate the situation to get the agreement settled. Unfortunately the Deputy had been on this coalface not such a long time before that so he had a good idea that this was nothing more than a puddle, and not the kind of perilous environment that was being described to him that would mean we all would end up soaked to the bone. The Deputy was clearly putting up some resistance, so the negotiation dragged on, all during the overtime, and so no work was getting done while this went on. However, on both sides of this discussion there was more at stake than a few pence per hour on the pay rate. It was a pride thing. Both were intent on proving their power and prowess as negotiators, able to get what they want when they want it. Unfortunately on this occasion the case for the extra money was just too weak so in the end this guy came grudgingly back to us, a little deflated by the defeat, and announced the verdict, which was – 'sorry lads, the gaffers have shat on us again' (shat being the colloquial past tense word for the normal bodily function).

It is my contention that it is this kind of standoff that was partly responsible for the development of the mining culture that would amuse me so much. The further north you got towards Yorkshire, the more prevalent that kind of culture would get. The end result of that is nobody readily admits to satisfaction of any kind because by doing that you may well be selling yourself short by surrendering an otherwise useful negotiating position where you got to have a good old moan and make your case for some kind of compensation. That same culture then developed beyond the mines and basically became the natural way of the whole mining community. So, if you ever asked a Yorkshire man if he liked something, the best answer you would ever expect to get was 'I've had worse'. That meant he really liked it, but you had to be familiar with the culture to understand that. There's no wonder that 'southerners' thought of the north to be a foreign land.

Of course different cultures are something you find everywhere. I particularly like a story I heard of a ship's captain who realised his ship was sinking and he took the decision to get all of his passengers to safety by jumping over the side and abandoning the boat. There were lots of different nationalities on board at the time. After trying his best he couldn't get them to jump off and exasperated he returned to the ship's cabin and instructed his second in command to see if he could do any better and persuade them to jump off. Fifteen minutes later he came back and reported to the Captain 'that's it Captain they're all off'. The Captain was astonished and said 'how did you do it?' to which he responded,

'Well, I told the English it would be proper to jump, so they jumped.'

'I told the French it would be stylish to jump, so they jumped.'

'I commanded the Germans to jump, so they jumped.'

'I told the Italians not to jump, so they jumped.'

'And I dared the Irish to jump, so they jumped.'

Then when the Captain realised all the passengers were off the ship, as an American he remembered the ship was insured so finally he also jumped.

It's a great story of the different cultures, with more than a little truth to it, but it also reflects the thing I have been saying all along about the different cultures of mines, and the fact that the management always had to be aware of the culture they were dealing with when it came to managing it if they wanted to make progress.

CHAPTER 31

So now we are into the topic of culture it brings me to the underlying issues that all communities face. Not just of diverse cultures, but also of race and religion. These can be hot topics nowadays, and quite sensitive, but they are key to understanding cultures and any organisation that brings them together which mining certainly does.

Of course miners never really felt too compelled to comply with pressures of political correctness so you shouldn't expect my experience of the past to comply too much with modern viewpoints. In more recent days things have changed a bit, especially with the emergence of social media which didn't exist back then even though it is not so long ago. Again I marvel at how much the world has changed in such a short time. To emphasise that point I clearly remember the time in the mix-sixties when I was a child; we neither has a television or a telephone. Certainly others had a television earlier than we did, which only arrived for me when I was aged eight. I will explain the reason for that shortly, but the telephone was also quite a late arrival for many of us in the village and I remember it as a real life changing event for us when it arrived. I can't remember what age that was but I was old enough to use it so it was around the mid-sixties at the earliest. Before that if there was an emergency of some kind and you needed the emergency services you would rush to the nearest neighbour's house where you knew they had a telephone.

When our telephone finally arrived we were assigned the number 'Edwinstowe 619'. That tells us a few things. First we had a local village exchange. Secondly there were only a little over five hundred telephones in the village at that time. And thirdly the exchange could only handle a maximum of 1000 telephones so that was the limit of the vision for our communication network at that point. Considering that now most teenagers and some children have a mobile phone and supercomputer in their pocket, the world has probably seen the biggest revolution of all time there, even before we discuss the internet. Eventually the local exchange was moved to Mansfield, a town ten miles away, and the numbers expanded to six figures. But not too long ago I discovered there is a village only a few miles away where at least until recently they retained their three figure numbers – the village of Caunton. I once rang a number there asking for someone I knew called Adrian but accidentally got the wrong number, even though it was only three figures. It turned out an Adrian did live at that number but he wasn't the one I was looking for. However he knew the guy I wanted and was able and happy to give me his number, which seemed rather bizarre. I guess that's village life for you. Maybe all the guys in that village are named Adrian?

With television my friends in the village already had a black and white TV, but one thing I have not really covered so far about the particulars of my upbringing is that my parents differed from the norm to some extent by the fact they were religious, which probably explains their desire for a big family. They were not the normal local Church of England types though, but belonged to a denomination that at one time would have been regarded as 'non-conformist'. They were quite serious and strict about all that too, so I was raised with it, and there were some strict rules to it. One was a negative view of television which was treated with a certain amount of suspicion and thought of by some that it could be a thing of the devil. We did have a Radiogram so we could listen to the radio or play vinyl records, but no TV. However, when I reached age eight everybody got the new-fangled colour TVs that were now available and my parents took the step of getting a black and white TV. Clearly the values had changed somewhat and only the colour TVs were now of the devil but the black and white ones were ok. Funny that!

In hindsight I was glad of no TV in my early years because I enjoyed a creative life and a life outdoors instead. When it came it certainly changed things a bit for us, though even the normal programmes like Doctor Who and the Daleks completely terrified me at first when I was not used to it. I think this concerned my parents so they came up with another strict rule which was no TV on Sundays. We already had a strict rule of no shopping on Sunday and no work, which made no difference anyway because back then the shops never did open on Sunday. The Sabbath at that time was pretty much observed by all, whether religious or not.

The 'no TV' on Sunday rule did cause me a particular dilemma because my favourite programme was Batman and Robin, which was a comedy but as a young lad it was all serious stuff to me. The problem was each story covered two episodes where the first was shown on Saturday and the Dynamic Duo always got themselves into some life threatening, perilous trouble, all instigated by one of the four regular baddies. Then on Sunday they would get out of their life threatening situation with a Houdini type of escape that I could never see coming. The trouble was I only ever saw them get into trouble and never saw them get back out of it, but they always turned up for the next episode the next weekend so they did clearly survive. I could have gone to a friend's house to see it; there were quite a few of my classmates that lived on my road – Dale, David, Glynn, Stephen and Martin. I always spent time at Dale's house reading his Beano comics with him so he wouldn't have minded at all, I'm sure. In fact in later years Dale's Mum pointed out to my daughter a small footprint in their concrete path and told her it was mine. I have apologised for that since but I reckon I got the idea for that kind of misdemeanour from reading Dennis the Menace at their house. Anyway, I didn't go there to see Batman because I was trying to keep to the rules of my parents feeling it must be quite important given they were so serious about it. Not all my brothers felt the same though. One of them confessed to running out of the house sometimes and shouting 'bum, bum, bum' and all the other words he knew he wasn't allowed to say, just to get rid of his frustration at all the damn rules. Though I was trying to comply I remember once sneaking over to a neighbour's house on Sunday to try to see the outcome of the previous day's Batman episode through the lounge window, desperate to see how they got out of the quicksand, or escaped the teeth of the shark or whatever, but it was difficult to work out what was happening without the sound, and I would always get a huge pang of guilt for disobeying my parents, especially when my brothers shopped me to them for watching TV on Sunday. I still say today that one day I am going to sit down and watch all those old episodes to see their escapes and I think it might turn out to be real healing therapy for me, releasing all that pent up tension I built up over those years wondering if or how they would escape.

One other thing I felt I missed out on was the yearly pit trip to the seaside where the whole village seemed to disappear on their annual trip on the train to the seaside at Skegness. I probably could have gone on the trip as my parents would have been able to get tickets from friends, or I could have gone with a friend who had a parent who was a miner, but the problem was again that it happened on Sunday and that didn't fit my parent's values. Instead I would stay behind and roam the village on that day knowing all my friends were at the seaside, still with no Batman and Robin as a consolation, not even through the windows.

When I grew to the point of making up my own mind about religion I wandered away from all that for a while, but I did pick some things up that stuck with me and the thing that brought it back later on was when I first began a career as a miner. I think it was looking at the life of the typical miner and asking the old questions of what it was all about, so at that point I began my own journey of faith again. That said, I am to this day reluctant to call it religious because I find though most people with no religion look at anyone who has faith as religious, for 'religious' people themselves I find the greater part of the challenge with it is to separate out the religious elements from their faith so it is a very personal walk of faith and pursuit of truth without the religious trappings to it. For a while that was a psychological battle for me that can only really be appreciated by those that have gone through it. I find in the English coal mines that is not the norm – many miners in my region were either atheist, agnostic or even cynical about religion, which I fully understand. However in other coalfields like Wales and Scotland the story is very different. Those communities tend to have a deep religious element to them that is not always appreciated by the coalfields of Nottinghamshire and other areas of England. It may have something to do with the fact that life in those Welsh and Scottish mines was considerably more difficult than the rest due to the incredibly low coal seams they worked and the hard conditions that I spoke about earlier. That may have had an effect like it did for the Negro slaves in the USA where life was so hard they came to seek a higher meaning to it all and so we get the old Negro Spiritual music developing, and song genres like gospel and the blues that would often be like a groaning for a better life than the one they knew, or for some justice for their cause. I remember visiting a Welsh church to hear a choir that were exactly this kind of thing where the song harped back to their younger days to a house on a snowy hillside where they were raised, wishing to return to be with their parents again who loved and cared for them as a child. It was very bluesy, and deeply moving, written as an expression of a deep desire for release from a hard life.

At times I visited mining machinery manufacturers like Anderson Strathclyde based in Motherwell, Scotland and I got a revelation about how deeply religion is bound to the culture up there. Of course I knew of the Catholic/Protestant troubles in Northern Ireland and have since seen the communities where the entrance to the village is painted orange to warn Catholics it was a Protestant village and so therefore to stay away. Of course what put all that in the news was the violence accompanying it back in those days, but it surprised me to find the same kind of thing going on in Scotland even if it was without the violence. To some degree it was common knowledge through the football teams in Glasgow nearby, where Celtic was predominantly Catholic, and Rangers Protestant – sectarianism on the terraces. What surprised me most was visiting the manufacturing works and discovering the factories were similarly segregated by religious persuasion. Motherwell is known as the Hallelujah town because of the level of religion there and I heard the stories of how Catholic or Protestant councillors would get the upper hand and then use their power to give favours to those of their own persuasion. It is all of this messy religious stuff that I found I had to dump for myself and retain those things in it that really mattered. While in Scotland I visited a few churches whilst up there in the industry as part of my training and saw the many different streams, including those that didn't really fall into either of those main categories but were more 'non-conformist' types like the thing I was raised in.

Not many in my village or area were religious but there were certainly many that had their personal beliefs that they generally kept to themselves. My Grandmother Swanwick was like that. She had a Bible which she read frequently but didn't attend church unless it was some special occasion. My Grandad was more concerned with his image and so didn't admit to much on that score; that is until he had some kind of personal experience in his last years when he was on his deathbed, but he found it difficult to speak about it, though it clearly really affected him. My faith includes great hope for them after seeing Grandad have that experience, then only six weeks after he died my Grandma followed him after we saw her have a special experience in a church one evening that she attended for a short while after Grandad's death. Sometimes those meetings seemed to get into a higher realm and that is what happened for her the night before she left us.

Not many miners I meet in my area are aware of some of the background with religion in other coalfields like the coal mines in the valleys of South Wales. At times the domestic conditions got really bad there, and then on the back of that there was a religious revival. As a result, in some of the villages in the Welsh valleys every tenth building is a church along the main road through the valley as a legacy to the days of revival. It is particularly those times in those mining communities where the marvellous singing skills and traditions of the Welsh people developed, much like those old Negro Spirituals of the slaves in the USA Deep South I mentioned earlier. Where conditions are bad these things often seem to go together to give a ray of hope to those that live such a harsh life, and the mines of Wales were certainly that. Anyway, as I was saying, when this religious revival took place in Wales around 1904 to 1907 it was the early days before mechanisation so the coal was transported underground by pit ponies rather than machines. During this time there was a problem getting the pit ponies to respond to commands because the miners suddenly stopped swearing and the ponies no longer understood their commands – a simple fact I just found rather amusing.

Those religious revivals came and went but they left a deep impression on the culture of those communities that has lasted to this day. For myself I already wrote a bit about my outlook on life and my faith after the many experiences I had, both good and bad. I have been walking that journey of faith for 40 years now and in that time have seen some incredible things; physical things, especially in the last 15 years. Things that are off the map for most people. In fact I have heard of even more remarkable things from sources I completely trust, so for that and other reasons my faith has held strong and so has that outlook of the possibility of life beyond where I will see my grandparents again, which makes me quite an optimistic person.

Getting back to the mines, in Nottinghamshire there was a considerable influx of Geordie miners from the North of England who were offered jobs in the new coalfields when the northern mines were closed through exhaustion. There is a saying about how wrong or ridiculous a thing is that says it's like 'sending snow to the Eskimos', or 'sending coals to Newcastle' meaning that Newcastle was at one time seen to be the very home of coal. Slowly those mines in the north began to close and the miners headed south.

Geordies in my eyes always proved to be lovely people; very warm, larger than life, and full of fun and passion. It is an amazing place to go as all the guys there call you 'man' and the women call you 'pet'. I have always said the further north you go in England the friendlier the people are. My family name does in fact have a strong presence up there so I am sure I have links there from past generations, which may be why I feel so at home when I go there. Their language also has that endemic comedy element you get with some British accents which always seems to me to give them a head start when it comes to entertainment value. In fact the whole humour of Geordie Land bears the hallmarks of what I know to be pit humour, which I would define to a large degree using another term I heard once – 'oppositional humour'. It is the same humour I have been sharing all along from the mines. It has a challenging, i.e. oppositional element to it. Take the Geordie's signature phase 'Wae'aye man' that I mentioned earlier. Translated that means 'yes', just like the Nottinghamshire and Derbyshire 'Eyup duck' means 'hello'. But actually 'Wae'aye man' means a whole lot more than that. First of all they added the 'man' on the end, which they always do endearingly whenever they speak to you, but the whole phase has that oppositional element embedded in it so what it really says in queen's English is 'Well of course you idiot, didn't you know that?' So it contains a subtle endearing insult that suggests you're a really thick idiot for not even knowing something so self-evident already – and all this fits into such a short expression that has more or less turned into a new word. How can you fail to love such a rich language as that? It's on a par with a new American word I discovered in South Carolina – the word 'wijadija'. A typical usage would be – 'You brought y'ur truck wijadija'. Language is culture, you must admit.

Of course Geordies are well and truly English despite the fact over history the border has shunted back and forth many times, sometimes as far south as York. There is actually a misconception with the Scots about their ongoing conflict with the English over the centuries before we formed the union. That is that the English were always the big aggressor with the huge population and armies that oppressed the Scots like big bullies. But when you look back in history it was actually much more of a fair fight back then because the populations of England and Scotland up to the potato famines in the nineteen century were very similar. Then if the Scots made an alliance with France or another enemy it meant England was in real trouble, as happened during the reign of Elizabeth I as queen of England. Now the numbers are something like 80% English to about 10% Scots in the UK, so they are a minority, rather than the near 50/50% or 55/45% it was back then, but it was not always like that.

Anyway, the reason I said all that was simply to say I didn't meet nearly as many miners in Nottinghamshire from Scottish or Welsh mines. I think it would be a bigger move for them because they love their countries and their culture and making the transition to the Midlands culture was probably a step too far for most of them to be happy, as it probably would be for English heading there. Also the regions they live in are beautiful countryside so I think few miners from there would want to leave all that. That said my best friend from school, Colin, was a miner's kid from Ayrshire. When he spoke to me it was perfect midlands English – a contradiction in terms I know – but when he spoke to his parents his accent was so thick I could hardly understand him, and they had been in England for many years. The accents were so wide apart it was like Colin had to be multi-lingual. As I said earlier, when you go to visit mining communities you find their isolation over the centuries has made their accents even broader than the norm.

Of course miners just saw any kind of accent, race, and religion as fair game for a laugh. In truth any difference they could fix on would be considered useful as bait. If you were the sort to react or show any outrage then you were fair game so their oppositional humour, as I called it, would immediately kick in.

That brings me to the whole issue of race in the mines. There were quite a few white Polish around. I once witnessed the pit men picking on one of them by suggesting Hitler invaded Poland at dinnertime and they were all in the Brown Cow pub in Mansfield by teatime. Not fair of course because the Poles did remarkable service for us in the war, not least in the RAF.

In my time as a child I was only aware of one family of any other colour than white in the neighbourhood who originally came from Jamaica, other than one family that came for a brief time of Asian/Indian origin from Uganda when Idi Amin scandalously kicked them out of Uganda after confiscating all their property. When I went to university in later years I had another friend who was an Indian Muslim that was kicked out at the same time and they went from land owners with servants in Uganda, to his Dad working manually in the steelworks at Scunthorpe. That family didn't stay long in the village, but the Jamaicans did and raised their own family there. Of course all of us who have lived in the village for any length of time know who I mean; many of them are still around. In later times I came to reflect on how courageous it was for their parents to come to the village when there were no others around of the same origins or race. I lived in

London for a while near Wembley where there are many different races and not many whites. And the whites that are there are mostly of other origins; many of them East Europeans. I realised how difficult and isolating that can be so to be a single Jamaican family in a village where all are mostly White British takes some strength of character. What I discovered is they were just about the friendliest people you could ever meet; always happy with time to talk to anybody that was prepared to pass the time of day with them. The father worked in the mine and at least two of his sons followed. The younger of these two was in my class at school from very early on so he became a friend, as he did with everybody else. He was a tough guy but of happy disposition like his Dad and not really the type to create trouble. His brother was a year or two older and physically tall and well built. He looked like a boxer. For that reason alone my friend in my school year was never likely to get any trouble at school while his older brother was around to back him up. That's just school for you, especially in a mining community. The same was true for my younger brothers as I was at the older end of my family. I got all the trouble and so got a bit of a reputation at times, even though my parents would give me hell if they heard of me involved in anything like that, given their values. They didn't really realise how hard it was to avoid trouble and survive in that environment. My brothers after me by contrast got relatively little trouble, again all based on the fact they had big brothers to back them up. Coming back to the Jamaican family, the older brother could handle himself in a fight and he was head and shoulders above the rest of them. However, at school one day I do remember walking around a corner where there seemed to be a lot of noise and meeting a sight I've never forgotten. They were trying to give him the bumps. The bumps is something that happened to all of us on our birthday where they grab you by your arms and legs and bump you on the ground once for each year of your age. It beat candles by miles for the fun, but it was a terrifying prospect for some so they desperately tried to keep their birthdate a secret, or played truant on that day, which didn't always work because they would be waiting for you the day after. When they discovered the birthday of my Jamaican friend's elder brother they were determined to get him but it took just about the whole of his school year to get the better of him. He wasn't too pleased about it and fought back like a superhero but that was the one time I saw them manage to do it. He too was a nice guy and didn't deserve it, but neither did the rest of us. Fortunately for me I got away with that and never had the bumps because my birthday landed in the summer holidays – something one or two of my friends were not too pleased about after their personal traumas.

For the Dad of my Jamaican friend to come here to England must have been a huge cultural shift. Even losing the sunshine is a big deal, but at least down the pit he would be back in the heat. No doubt the men would have tried the usual baiting based on race, I can't be sure, I never saw or heard it, but they certainly became respected hard workers down there. I guess their physicality alone would have been enough to command respect, but let's face it, after a couple of hours working down a mine in that heat everyone was pretty much the same colour anyway. They are all still valued and respected members of the local community today. I happened to drive past my old friend just the other day walking along the pavement and he looked as happy as ever.

For me my equivalent Achilles heel was probably my faith, or religion. Most people kept quiet about it but my background and that of a few others in the pit was to be open to speak about it if people asked, so naturally that 'weakness' got out and made me a target for baiting and fun whenever we had a spare moment and they got the chance. I am certain at times they spent every spare moment thinking up what to say to me next that might wind me up and get a reaction because they would show up each time with some really creative comments or jokes.

There were the old ones like – there were cars in the Bible because it says Moses came down the mountain in his Triumph (that was a car make back then).

Or the time God said to Moses he had some commandments for him and Moses asked how much they cost. When God said nothing he said – yes please, I'll have ten.

But one of the best was about where in Genesis it says God said 'Let them come forth' but they came fifth and he lost his beer money.

In the end I decided to give away stickers as a reward for a good comments or a worthy joke, which was a smiley sunshine face with the words 'Smile Jesus Loves You' on it. After a while these stickers became all the rage at the mine so men would come asking me for them, even offering me cigarettes, despite the fact I didn't smoke. After a while most of the miners at the pit were wearing these stickers. That kept it all good humoured of course, but I still maintain to this day those stickers made the mine a happier place.

Whatever it was they chose to pick on, all of this banter served to entrench the mining culture and make miners the breed they are, with their thick rhino hides and their oppositional humour. These are the ways that British southerners with their niceties seem to be so often mystified by.

CHAPTER 32

Amid the ongoing pressures of the serious business of keeping coal flowing from a mine and all the work that takes, the pranksters among the miners and technicians would always find time to make some sport, usually at the expense of one or more of their fellow workers. Take for example the occasion in the surface vehicle maintenance garage when one of the mechanics decided to wire the vehicle ignition system electrics to the garage work bench. Then, at a key moment, when his workmates were well into a something on the bench, he would throw a switch and give them all an electric shock like the ones animals get from an electric boundary fence – enough to make you jump. Of course after this happened a couple of times they went looking for the cause and found the wiring leading straight back to the vehicle the culprit was busy fixing. His punishment was a broomstick through the sleeves of his overalls and then hoisted up to dangle in the workshop for the whole of snap time. That would certainly serve to even up the bragging rights and humiliation that would follow at the welfare after such a prank.

Then there was the initiation ceremony for new apprentice mechanics in the loco garage, which was to be covered with grease and thrown into the sand pit – only then could he be accepted into the fold.

In the pit baths I frequently saw the old shower trick where a lad is trying to get bathed and off home but his mates are feeding lashings of shampoo into his shower stream so the whole cubicle is full of suds. Of course he would know what was happening – it was an old trick, so he would be screaming obscenities at them to make them stop, but would be at their mercy with his face and eyes full of soap suds. Of course all this is not exclusive to the mines. In my college years some student friends of mine took to drilling chalk and inserting a live match in the hole so when the lecturer got into full flow writing on the chalk board it would ignite. The different responses you got to that were fascinating – ranging from the jump and scream, to the one that held it up as it burned and with astonishment said 'these are made from gypsum aren't they', to the one that casually said 'I didn't realise I was writing that fast', and just swapped it for another stick, which was also drilled and loaded, it so happened.

On that score I have a confession to make from my mid teenage years. One day I was out with a few friends who were fellow enthusiast with the birds of prey. We walked for miles in the country and came to the gate of a huge field we needed to cross, but it was full of bullocks – that's bulls less a couple of anatomical accessories. They can sometimes be very frisky and curious animals and so gathered around the gate blocking our path. I was used to them having worked on a local farm during the harvest so I jumped in and shooed them off, to which the herd just parted. My friends, Garry, Ian and Benny, however, were not so experienced and were understandably very cautious, especially given that two of them were quite a bit smaller than me. For about ten minutes I stood in the field with the cows and assured them we could walk across the field slowly and calmly and the cows would just let us pass – no problem. Eventually they plucked up courage and at first they did as I had instructed – walk calmly, don't run, all stay together, just ignore the cows. But then they got a bit unnerved by the warm breath they could feel of the cows from following us very closely, so they began to scurry and leave me behind, all the time with me telling them to just slow down. Of course they didn't listen and I started to feel a bit of injustice to be left with the whole herd of cows behind me and my friends about 20 metres ahead. It was then I had the dastardly idea. I ran as silently as I could and then as I passed them at high speed I yelled 'run, they're coming'. My head start on them meant I got to the boundary fence first and had time to turn and watch what was going on behind me. There were my (former) friends running as fast as their legs would take them, with eyes as wide as saucers, and cows running behind them so closely they could feel their breath on the backs of their necks. They looked absolutely terrified, but in fact the cows behind them weren't even breaking a sweat, they were just keeping up wondering what all the fuss was about. Benny was a particularly small lad. When he finally reached the boundary with a cow still right behind him in hot pursuit, he dived headlong into a prickly hawthorn hedge to escape. I laughed a lot, but years later I felt quite guilty when I found out cows can actually be very dangerous, though only usually when there is a dog and they have calves they want to protect. In any case I decided to write this one up as a confession to BBC Radio 2. I'm not sure if they ever used it, or if I was in fact forgiven, but I think my friends did forgive me once they realised they'd survived, even though I don't remember ever crossing a field of cows like that with them again. I don't know if these antics could be considered 'horse play' as it clearly only involved cows on this occasion, not horses.

CHAPTER 33

The pressures of a mine could be extremely demanding for the managers and engineers who had overall responsibility, especially if the general pit Manager was the tyrannical type. I remember an Electrical Engineer over a mine telling me how it absorbed his whole life day and night. This was in the days before mobile phones. He would often get a phone called at home in the middle of the night demanding his urgent attention to manage the situation whenever the mine broke down. For some mines that was a very frequent thing. If the engineer was off duty and not at home the manager would send out van drivers to find him. He told me the last straw came when he was standing at the edge of a pond in his waders fishing and the van driver tapped him on the shoulder. Once found there was no escape, he had to drop what he was doing and go to the mine. I asked him how he coped with that kind of pressure. He said 'I go sea fishing now'. I fully understand the pressures having been a shift charge engineer on nights at Mansfield Colliery. One night all five seams broke down together. I had to get everybody I could muster out of bed, otherwise the cost to the mine would be immense. Believe me it's not the kind of pressure you ever forget.

When I completed my years of study, as a university postgraduate I moved on to the next phase of my training to be a manager in the mines with a course that led me into greater positions of responsibility managing shifts in the mechanical department, managing projects at the various mines for a time, and attending courses along with my colleagues that were designed to develop our management skills ready for taking full responsibility. During this time we all had to deliver lectures on aspects of the industry to both our colleagues and area level high ranking management. I chose to study the whole fundamental purpose of mining, which is to produce energy, and to ask and answer the question of just how much energy we have to expend to mine the coal that in the end we use to generate energy for others.

To begin with I had no idea of the answer to that. It could have been anything from 1% or less, to 50% or more of the energy in the coal we mined that was expended to actually mine it – I just didn't know. I was aware of a problem in the USA where the huge steam locomotives would haul the coal halfway across the country for it to be used, and it was discovered that these locos burned a huge proportion of the coal just by making the journey because they were so inefficient and it was so far – sometimes as much as 40% of production I believe. In later years I once visited the Ford Motor Museum in Detroit – a fascinating place. There I noticed a strange black wall of pipes that looked like something I imagine from an old gasworks factory. I then realised the wall had wheels and as I stood back a bit I realised it was one of these massive coal hauling steam locos. What a monster it was. It was worth visiting the museum just to see it. No wonder they burned coal at an awesome rate. Of course part of the problem would be the loco would be up and down inclines as the track passed over hills, which would all waste fuel. They were forced to take a serious look at economy for the transport or simply risk their mining ventures to become unprofitable, which for them would certainly bring the industry to a swift end.

For the UK we had an additional problem. Ours are deep mines, whereas in the USA they are mostly opencast so they basically just uncover the coal and scoop it up off the floor. We have to wind all of the coal up a shaft for as much as a whole kilometre just to get it to the surface, all of which requires energy. One thing I still find incredible was that Ollerton Colliery and others in the Nottinghamshire area were still running winding engines that were steam powered up until my time. In fact the waste hot water from the steam engines was used to provide central heating to the pit village houses – a radical and advanced idea at the time. Sometimes when the engine was not producing enough hot water to serve the needs of the village the winder would get a call to stoke the boilers to release more hot water. The supply was simply part of the deal for the miners renting the houses.

Waste hot water like this does sound like an inefficiency, but actually, though not everybody understands it, it was and is unavoidable. Like Newton's laws of gravity and motion, there are other natural scientific laws concerning the conversion of heat to work energy. The first law of thermodynamics says both heat and work are energy, so it is only possible to get the same amount of work energy as the heat – i.e. there is a one to one conversion. However, the second law of thermodynamics basically says, if we want to convert heat energy to work energy there must be waste heat, and it is impossible to convert it all. Of course I'm paraphrasing it there, but that is what it says. That means when we want to burn coal to drive a steam engine to haul a load like in a loco, or to wind it up a shaft, we have to waste a proportion of the heat. We can still use it as heat, but we can't convert it all to work. The same principle is true of our modern power stations because electricity is actually work energy, but the waste heat doesn't get used as it did at the colliery; it goes into the environment somehow – usually the river or the atmosphere.

With electricity electrons are shunted back and forth along a cable as work energy. The waste heat during conversion of coal to electricity is why we need cooling towers and why we raise the river temperature by a few degrees so even tropical fish are happy living in it near the power station. So winding coal is a big energy user, but so are all the materials we require for mining. Everything we use has to be made using energy, especially metal items like steel. Then there is the underground haulage of men and supplies to the coalfaces, and the conveyors that carry the coal through miles of roadway back to the pit bottom. For the steam winders there was lots of waste energy due to inefficiency like the locos, but once they became electric the amount of electrical energy needed is actually very close to exactly what it takes to lift the coal load by that distance – the electrical winding engines are about as efficient as they can be, even feeding electricity back into the system at some points of the wind when a load is descending, or when the ascending load is slowing down.

In the end the figure I came up with as the nearest overall estimate I could make was 5%. We use 5% of the energy of the coal we mine to actually mine it and get it to the pit surface, which is not bad, all things considered. There is certainly room there to make a profit. From that point it has to be hauled to the power station and then used to drive the steam turbines. The surface railways are virtually level and the power station is relatively near so the losses are as low as they could be for the haulage. The efficiency of power stations is another matter. Producing electricity this way is convenient, but not necessarily efficient. Ratcliffe power station near Nottingham was one of the most efficient at a thermal efficiency of 32%. The rest went into the atmosphere or the river as heat. Then there are the losses from transmitting the electricity through the electricity grid which brings the efficiency down to about 25% by the time it finally reaches the consumer. Then of course there is the inefficiency of the devices we use it on, and if electricity is used for heat that is really quite wasteful given that heat was already wasted to produce it. In these days where we have global warming issues this seems scandalous, but part of it is a natural and inevitable cost of producing energy, made worse by producing it in a centralised way like this.

CHAPTER 34

At one mine where I worked the undermanager had a management problem developing of miners always seeming to get injured on the afternoon shift at about the same time in the evening. After a while someone spotted the trend. It always happened when there was a big football match on TV. Of course these guys were making it home in time for the match. The remedy was to always take them to the hospital for a thorough examination so they ended up waiting long hours to be seen by the doctor, which seemed to miraculously cure the problem. After that there would be a steady stream of other excuses rather than injuries, but like school, when their grandmother has died for the third time you start to get a bit suspicious. There was always a real audacity to it when it was the same roguish characters every time pulling the same stunt. The managers just had to play the cat and mouse game of management vs men to try to handle it. Once again for some it was part of their legend at the pit to get away with that kind of thing, and they would often be heard bragging about it at the Miner's Welfare later the same evening. I suppose life is just a game from end to end for some. Thankfully many others took the job more seriously and we did actually find some coal down there.

Speaking of audacity, I always did think the whole idea of undermining everybody's land and property to be an extremely audacious thing to do, no matter how deep below them you mine it. After all gravity only goes in one direction. I already wrote about the impact of subsidence and the cost to the industry once they finally had to pay for it. For the local mines of Thoresby, Ollerton and Bilsthorpe there were some notable cases of undermining that must have cost the industry dear. One was the subsidence crack that developed in the bed of Rufford Lake in the local country park. The lake just drained away into the substrata. It meant it was dry for a long time until the cracks were filled and repaired. Fortunately the whole area was later revamped and upgraded which made up for the loss, but it must have been costly for the industry.

The other local undermining that became a bit of a scandal was the damage done to Thoresby Hall, the local stately home on whose estate Thoresby Colliery was originally situated, which is why it was called Thoresby Colliery rather than Edwinstowe Colliery as originally intended. In the end the most economical option for the industry turned out to be to actually purchase the hall at a price of millions, so it was owned by British Coal for a while. No doubt had they not done that, and the estate had driven the legal demand for repairs, the cost would have been astronomical as it is a listed building of course, from the 18th century. It is now a beautiful Warner Holidays site so the story ends well, and the mine still seems to have profited by it, but I still see it as an extremely audacious thing for anywhere to be undermined without the consent of the owners, but that is what has happened over the years of mining. I guess in the end all these interests have had to give way to what is judged to be the national interest and that is the final justification for it.

During my time in the industry I achieved the qualifications needed to take charge of a UK mine as the Mechanical Engineer, but the industry in the UK began to close before there was any chance of me getting a posting. That means my engineer's ticket is only good for posterity now, or toilet paper I guess. In fact the global jobs pool was shrinking as the unprofitable mines were closed first in other parts of the country, so engineers were arriving to take the spare jobs, and jobs were even being invented in

Nottinghamshire to accommodate those who wanted to stay in the industry. For myself I could see the computer industry developing and from my time at university I decided I wanted to be a part of it, so I would be leaving mining in any case. I therefore became the very first person in management in Nottinghamshire to request and receive redundancy.

I made that request for redundancy in January 1988. The request had to go to national level for approval because if granted it would mark a change in policy for management, but four weeks later I received notice of approval and was asked what date I would like to leave. I chose the last day in March to coincide with the end of the tax year, and I got a rather surprised response from my line manager, who accepted my proposal, but I didn't understand his surprise and he wouldn't explain it. Then the following day, as I went into the Engineer's office at Mansfield Colliery where I was stationed and I was just about to tell my boss, the Mechanical Engineer, about my arrangement to leave when he suddenly said 'I have an important announcement, the pit is scheduled to close.' The men were really surprised because so far no pit had closed in Nottinghamshire. Their first question was 'When?' Without hesitation the answer came back 'The end of March'. I had chosen to leave the industry on the very day the pit I was working at was scheduled to close after a hundred years of working. Not only was it the first in Nottinghamshire, but no pit anywhere had closed in such a hurry, ever. The decision came from the fact that Mansfield Colliery had cost the industry vast sums in subsidence claims and was now trying to stay alive by using unconventional *Shortwall* mining methods to try to survive and at the same time trying to cause no more subsidence, but it was a risk and the claim was made that this strategy was not working. Everybody in the department believed I knew something prior to this because I was based at Area Headquarters rather the mine and had chosen to leave on the same day, but I actually knew nothing about it. I think even my line manager back at Area HQ thought I had an inside track somehow before the announcement, which was the reason for his surprise as at that time the pit closure was a closely guarded secret given that it could turn out to be highly political. British Coal senior management expected firm resistance to the closure. In the end extremely generous redundancy payments were offered to those who wanted it – enough for many older ones to retire, and jobs were offered at other mines for those who wanted to continue to work in the industry, so the resistance was not too great and the closure was accepted without too much trouble. I was at the meeting where the worried miners voiced their concerns to management, but in truth everyone knew the days of the UK coal industry were numbered and this pit would certainly be near the top of the list for closure in the area. After I left the industry my contemporaries from all departments came out in droves and went into every manner of job, from managers to airline pilots. They were fortunate to have qualifications that set them in good stead anywhere really.

Of course, since the closure of Mansfield Colliery all the other Nottinghamshire pits also closed and we have seen coal mining come to its final end in recent years with Thoresby Colliery closing in July 2015, no less than 90 years after the shafts were sunk. This was the last mine in the country to go, and quite rightly from my point of view as Thoresby was such a huge success it deserved to be last. Those that worked this mine have the right to be very proud. Of course the legacy all the mines have left us is the pit tip, or spoil heap. As a geek I sometimes reflect on the fact that the tips are usually many time larger than the

Egyptian pyramids and that is only a minor fraction of the material that has been extracted as the tip only represents the waste material and not the coal. That gives a real perspective on the scale of the coal mining industry.

Most tips were reasonably well placed to be less intrusive on communities, but rules and practices only developed slowly on this so some were much more unsightly and intrusive than others. I remember reading one famous writer, though I'm not sure who it was (maybe H. G. Wells), referring to Clipstone tip as a real carbuncle. It was one of those tips that was really huge due to the high level of waste rock content of the product from the mine. It was also very close and visible to the village for a long distance along the main road, so it was just hard to miss, and it committed the unforgivable sin of cutting the community off from easy access to the pine forest beyond. Since the closure of the mine at Clipstone in 2003 the tip has gone through some investment in reclamation so it is now an accessible and quite pleasant place to walk, though it is very difficult to disguise completely the fact any hill is really a spoil heap.

In Wales this is particularly true where the mines were even older. The same is true of the slate mines there of course, where there are fascinating roads that drive straight though the middle of a slate spoil heaps that look to me like it could slip and bury the road at any moment. I have no doubt they are actually quite safe, but my imagination can't help but suggest it when I pass though there, which makes it both an interesting and spine tingling drive. Of course Wales does have a legacy of coal pit tips slipping like this with the disaster at Aberfan that killed 144 people, burying a school full of children. It was one of those disasters that forced further changes in the law to make the tips safer. I think it is actually quite fortunate that the coal industry was nationalised in terms of this legacy of pit tips because it meant the standards for maintaining the environment were generally quite high. Much higher I think than it would have been under private industry. In many cases the worst tips do in fact stem back to the days before nationalisation in 1947. The best pit tip I ever saw was Bevercotes Colliery that really did excel in its planning and management because it was a relatively new mine in a remote area, beginning production in 1967 and closing in 1993. The tip is contoured in such a way that it is well disguised to be a natural hill. I spent some time with the surveyors there, during my training, making sure it conformed to the plans. That too is now a pleasant country park that is accessible to the public, so the legacy in that case is a good one. I will of course always remember that tip from the memorable day when a horde of marauding Yorkshire Zulu's came charging over the horizon, so my memories of it will always be fonder than most I guess.

That was the end of my experience in mining in 1988 and I went into engineering software development using my knowledge, experience and education in other ways. All of that academic and practical experience proved to be invaluable in my work in many ways, but of course it was an academic virtual world rather than a physical one, which proved to be something I missed and I had to find ways to compensate for it with outdoor activities and sport whenever I could.

Although the mining connection ended, there is an epilogue for me to all that. After twenty years of software development I was living in the city of Nottingham and I decided to seek funds from the government for an innovative research project developing some new electronic hardware. I wanted to create something physical rather than virtual like software for a change. I needed an office for the job and it turned out I could obtain higher research funds if I set up in a former mining area. That led me straight back to Edwinstowe and the former British Coal Nottinghamshire Area Headquarters offices in Edwinstowe House where I was always based and employed by while in the industry. It is now a business enterprise centre. The irony is the office I rented was on the same wing as the offices of my former bosses that I answered to throughout the latter years of my training, so I guess in some ways it felt like promotion, even though I was now working for myself. The project I took on there also had a local connection as it was a project to develop a targeting scope for an archery bow, similar to gun scope on a gun but with some quirky features that won it the award of grant funds available for innovation. The archery scope was able to make compensation for the drop of an arrow over distance allowing you to simply line up cross hairs on an electronic screen with a distant target and make an accurate shot. That was one feature, but the main one that got me the funds was a feature that allowed it to be used for fishing – or as it is called in the USA, bowfishing. The problem with bowfishing is refraction of light at the water surface, which means when you see a fish in the water it is not in the position that you see it because the light is bent as it exits the water. It is refraction that makes a stick look bent when you dip it in water. I found a way to make that compensation so again you could target the fish simply by aligning the cross hairs of the device with the underwater target, and I patented the invention. The device was intended for either use with a target, or for hunting in other countries; particularly the USA where the archery market is huge – 12 million archers. In the UK the use of a bow for fishing or hunting would be not be legal because here it is illegal to hunt anything with a bow. That goes back to English laws still in place that were never repealed since Robin Hood's times that make it illegal to shoot the Kings deer. Of course, as we know, that didn't stop Errol Flynn in that iconic Robin Hood scene where he forced his way into Nottingham Castle carrying a huge stag he had hunted with his bow, and then after considerable impudence towards the usurper of the crown, Prince John, he made a swashbuckling escape, again without pulling a single threat in his tights.

I guess that scene alone is what made our local legend global back in 1938, so maybe we are all really a bunch of outlaws at heart. If you don't identify with that then let me tell you there is yet another law, still not repealed, that demands every male of age 14 or over must do two hours of archery practice per week, and apparently if you live in York it is legal to shoot a Scotsman so long as it's not Sunday. Sorry to my Scottish friends for pointing that out; I think our countries joined forces since then so I don't think that still stands. In any case, like it or not, those laws make outlaws of a whole lot of us, unless of course you do happen to be an archery enthusiast and you get in two hours of practice or more each week. I suspect some of my ex-miner friends will be happy to wear that outlaw title as a badge of honour.

CHAPTER 35

As I get to the end of my meandering trip down memory lane I hope you enjoyed travelling it with me. As a former miner and engineer in the mines I am thinking about what I would like to be the final word on it all, like the closing ceremony of the Olympics where somebody has to lead the way and carry the flag. Who will that be?

There are many heroes I look back on, some of whom died for their cause to feed their family and provide energy for their nation. But for me, as these are my memoirs, there is one person to whom I feel I owe that accolade, and that is a former Overman from Thoresby Colliery by the name of Eric Swanwick who is, and always will be a hero in my eyes, and the best grandad I could have ever wished for. Of course there are many like him that go back as far as the days when mining was gruelling manual labour, when Eric was just a young man, but I choose him not just because he is my Grandad, but because he represents all those of our Olympic mining team of the past that risked their lives daily for their families and communities.

Eric was not one of those killed by an accident or disaster, but he died from pneumoconiosis, the infamous miner's lung disease. So to me he is still a martyr for his cause because I saw that suffering of his last days first hand. My mother, his daughter, and my brothers, his grandsons loved him absolutely – we always will, and I for one expect one day to meet him again. Life in this world is tough. All of us live and die, and we all see some kind of trouble through the span of it. If I had the chance would I change it all and opt for a life of comfort? That would be a hard question for me to answer for all. I guess for many it was so tough they would choose the easier life. But for me I was fortunate to see the better end of the industry and it made me who I am. I said it before, mining is not just a job, it is a way of life and it is a culture. One that for me leaves me with no regrets and I will always feel privileged and proud to have been a part of it.

TREVOR MADDISON